The More You Know

Getting the evidence

and support you need

to investigate a

troubled relationship

William F. Mitchell, Jr.

PRIVATE INVESTIGATOR

President, Mitchell Reports

EAGLE'S NEST PUBLICATIONS
Endwell, New York
2004

Cover artwork by Dunn + Associates, Hayward, WI, http://www.dunn-design.com
Cover writing by Susan Kendrick Writing, Hayward, WI

Published in the U.S.A by
Eagle's Nest Publications
P.O. Box 8735, Endwell, NY 13762-8735
Email:customerservice@eaglesnestpub.com
http://www.eaglesnestpub.com

ISBN: 0-9718645-0-0

Printed in the United States of America

Library of Congress Cataloging-in-Publication data available upon request from the publisher.

This book is available at quantity discounts for bulk purchases.
For information, call 1-800-785-2425.

Fictitious names are used in this book to protect the identities of those subject to investigation. When the author says women are victims, the references will identify perpetrators as "he" and victims as "she."

The author, William F. Mitchell, Jr., is available for a limited number of speaking engagements and consulting assignments. For more information visit www.eaglesnestpub.com

READERS ARE SAYING

"ANY HUSBAND OR WIFE who may benefit from proving adultery in divorce court should read this book by William F. Mitchell, Jr., and then run out a hire a private eye! I did on behalf of my client."

—ROBIN ROSHKIND, ESQUIRE, DIVORCE LAWYER, PALM BEACH, FLORIDA

"Q: Can you recommend any good book for helping me to determine if my spouse is involved in an affair? A: Yes, *The More You Know* by William F. Mitchell, Jr."

—GITLIN, HAAFF & KASPER, WOODSTOCK, IL

"It's never too late. The signs of adultery often precede the affair. If you recognize one or more of them in your spouse, do something about it if you want to save the marriage."

—FRANK J. LAROCCA, ESQUIRE, SPINATO, CONTE & LAROCCA, GLEN ROCK, NJ

"I'VE BEEN A DIVORCE LAWYER forty years and know what's for real and what isn't. Bill Mitchell's book is on the money. It's credible, accurate and very much for real. Mitchell is a true pro and it show. His ethics and integrity shine through on each and every page."

— J. RICHARD KULERSKI, ATTORNEY AT LAW, OAK BROOK, IL

"TO LIVE ENTANGLED IN LIES and deception consumes our energy and well being. Bill Mitchell in his new book, The More You Know, provides a valuable service by conveying the importance of seeking the truth. Bill uses his background as a detective to give you this gift."

—DR. ROBERT HUIZENGA, HTTP://WWW.BREAK-FREE-FROM-THE-AFFAIR.COM.

"WILLIAM F. MITCHELL, JR. is one of the most outstanding investigators in America today. He learned from the best, his father, William F. Mitchell, Sr., a former FBI Agent and close friend and confidante of mine. This book is a help to everyone in their every day life. It furnishes knowledge beyond just those experiencing this dilemma."

—TED GUNDERSON, SR. SPECIAL AGENT IN CHARGE OF LOS ANGELES-FBI RETIRED, AUTHOR "HOW TO LOCATE ANYONE WITHOUT LEAVING HOME" EP DUTTON, 1989 (28 YEARS WITH THE FBI AND 50 YEARS AS AN INVESTIGATOR), LECTURER AND JOURNALIST, BEVERLY HILLS, CALIFORNIA

"THROUGHOUT MY YEARS as an investigator and my involvement in the teaching industry I have read or reviewed literally hundreds of books and articles relating to the private investigation practice. Bill Mitchell has taken his years as an investigator and combined them with a heart of empathy and understanding for the emotional, life altering scenario simply known as adultery. His book will serve as an incredibly useful tool to investigators involved in this type of investigation, but more importantly it serves as a source of help for those that find themselves in the unfortunate situation of wondering if their spouse or significant other is being unfaithful. Thank you Bill for putting education and heart into your book."

—W. LARRY DAVIS, LAWRENCEVILLE, GEORGIA — PRIVATE INVESTIGATOR FOR TWENTY-ONE YEARS AND FORMER MARINE CRIMINAL INVESTIGATOR,

"I RECOMMEND THIS BOOK to my clients who suspect their spouses of infidelity. I keep copies in my waiting room and clients have found them informative and helpful."

—HARVEY C. SHAPIRO, ESQUIRE, MATRIMONIAL ATTORNEY, BINGHAMTON, NY

"THIS BOOK IS CLEAR, concise and very useful for anyone affected by infidelity. I would call the author 'the Dr. Phil' of detectives—he cuts to the chase. As a psychotherapist, I would recommend it to clients!"

—VIRGINIA, USA, MAY 20, 2002

"THE MORE YOU KNOW is written by experienced private investigator William F. Mitchell Jr. for the purpose of helping men and women of all ages and backgrounds who find themselves victimized by the adultery of their spouses, and can often find no tangible and thematically appropriate help in their personal and marital crisis. Mitchell offers a unique and "real world" based compendium of advice about the "warning signs of adultery", how to satisfy a "need to know"; how to resolve issues of adultery even before they start; how to "adultery proof" a marriage; and when adultery has occurred, how to save a marriage. The More You Know is one of those self-help books that we never want to have need of—but will find invaluable when we do."

—BOOK REVIEWS, BOOK LOVER RESOURCES, ADVICE FOR WRITERS AND PUBLISHERS HOME/INTERNET BOOKWATCH VOLUME 12, NUMBER 10 OCTOBER 2002 HOME | IBW INDEX - M AUGUST 9, 2002

"There are, of course, a lot of books 'out there' regarding the topic of adultery, but I think Mr. Mitchell's experience as a private investigator resulted in an exceptionally informative and easy-to-read book offering sound practical advice. A personal example. . . . I didn't read this book until AFTER confronting my husband . . . without 'proof.' Then I saw my very own situation reflected in Mr. Mitchell's book. Get the book, follow his advice. He really knows what he's talking about."

—M, AUGUST 9, 2002

"THE MORE YOU KNOW is worth its weight in gold and I highly value your opinion on this matter because of your extensive field experience and the obvious understanding you have regarding the devastation infidelity can cause. Thank you."

—MARY R, FLORIDA, JULY 9, 2003

ACKNOWLEDGEMENTS

The creation of a book can only be accomplished by many remarkable and talented people. I am extremely grateful to everyone who contributed to this work. They are:

First, I must thank Susan Kendrick of Susan Kendrick Writing and Kathleen Dunn of Dunn + Associates for their resourcefulness and talents. What an excellent job done and I truly enjoyed this phase of the project.

Second, an author must be edited, edited, edited ... and hopes to survive the ordeal. Authors are much better for it and so are their readers. Those who came to my rescue were my wife Linda, my daughter Rachel, Alice Caroompas, Jody & Daniel Farley, Esquire, Anne & Dr. Lynn Bayly, Taze Yanick, Karen Bernardo, Dayna Barnes, and Susan Kendrick.

Last and most important is the sacrifice made by my family, Linda, Rachel, William III, Jessica and Kimberly. I can't thank you enough for allowing me the time to complete this most important venture.

I am deeply appreciative for all your insights, efforts and contributions. You've made this book no longer just a dream but a reality.

This edition is a superb resource for those experiencing the pain of infidelity.

WILLIAM F. MITCHELL, JR.
ENDWELL, NY

DEDICATION

It is fitting for me to devote this work to my father, **WILLIAM F. MITCHELL, SR.**, who was so attentive to scores of excellent pursuits and performed all of them extremely well.

Dad you are remarkable.
I love you.

CONTENTS

INTRODUCTION

In this age of rampant divorce, the number of adultery victims is on the rise. Fifty percent of all marriages now end in divorce. Amazingly, partners in dating relationships now turn to investigative services like mine. In recent years I've witnessed Internet-aided adultery. Partners start in chat rooms making contacts. They then use E-mail to carry out their plans. Eventually they rendezvous and commit adultery.

On average, adulterous relationships last a few months to half a year; yet the effects can last a lifetime. That is why we recommend our clients work quickly to obtain evidence when adultery is suspected.

I wrote this book to provide information as a means of dealing with adultery. My goal is to improve your chances of beating the odds and saving your marriage. If you must resort to the courts, then obtaining proof is vital to you. Your marital assets stand in the balance. This book offers ways to recognize if your partner is committing adultery. I reveal common behavior, telltale signs, and indicators of adultery. They do not differ just because you live in a particular area. I submit that unfaithful partners everywhere behave in much the same way. Some adulterers are more clever and cunning, while others are careless, but normally the same techniques can be employed to shed light on their activities.

Many factors must be considered as you decide how to handle your own situation. Initially upon suspecting a problem, the victim of adultery must act thoughtfully, quickly and silently. You will need to make choices, especially whether to continue sexual relations with your spouse, given the many sexually transmitted diseases today.

In my thirty years of practice, I've helped many clients deal with choices they were forced into making. In the midst of this crisis, victims need someone they can trust and talk to about their future. I've been that person. From this vantage point I know how troubling adultery can be for them. From my experience, many men fall victim to adultery, but overwhelmingly the victims are women.

Before leaving this introduction, I would like to try to establish a foundation for this book. By describing a healthy marriage, we establish a basis for early detection of infidelity. Why? It is for the same reason bank tellers study real money. They repeatedly handle authentic dollars until finding the counterfeit becomes easy. The better they know the real thing, the more likely they are to recognize the phonies.

A healthy marriage has positive attributes. We want a marriage where a solid union exists. We need to love each other, share intimacy, enjoy common beliefs and values, stay within boundaries, and talk. As this marriage continues to mature, couples learn to live in harmony and love. Let's explore this idea.

First, communication is vital. Discussing any subject is normal. Issues of sex, love, money, kids, purchases, and plans should get discussed openly. Healthy partners are committed to talking things through. I once heard a speaker jokingly say, "My wife and I never fight, but neighbors can hear us reasoning for miles." Marriages with good communications stay strong.

Second, flourishing marriages are made up of partners who trust each other. Trust bonds husbands and wives. It is essential. Marriages suffer when unfaithful partners violate trust. When trust is violated, it is like a fabric being torn in half or a beautiful artwork defaced. You will always wonder - is he being honest? Did he really go there? This lack of trust creates stress. It can lead to doubting your spouse's every move.

Third, marriage partners who work on their marriages reap the rewards. When they spend their time working with each other, they will not drift apart. These marriages last for decades as the couple enjoys their children and share memories together in their golden years.

No one has a perfect marriage, but when trouble comes, healthy partners look for answers to their problems. They don't run from them, but resolve them.

Lastly, love is the strength of marriage. Love covers many shortcomings. Without love a marriage fails to flourish.

I professionally witnessed my first case of adultery at age seventeen. I realized then just how risky this type of work would be. My assignment was to follow a couple during a lunch hour. I saw them meet just before she got in his car. Then I followed them through heavy traffic and many red lights. The surveillance ended at a deserted manufacturing site on a dead end street. This was a high crime area. With my blood pressure rising, I was scared and alone. To make matters worse, I had no other option but to crawl through a field, lugging a large 16mm camera. To get the proof I needed, my only choice was to climb a tree and take film of the two in his car. The whole time, I did not want to get caught. I was in a very dangerous place. The nearest pay phone was blocks away. In that neighborhood, finding a phone that worked was difficult. I thought at that moment, "What if this guy sees me?" Well, he didn't, and I safely returned to the office unscathed, retaining proof of this rendezvous.

It's not always this challenging, but that was my first experience. This day left an impression on me that I will not forget. Since then, I have traveled thousands of miles and conducted countless hours of surveillance obtaining evidence. I've testified in many courtrooms. Judges have ruled in my clients' favor nearly 100 percent of the time. My success resulted from great personal commitment and sacrifice. Clients frequently called at the most inconvenient times, like 2:00 a.m. or in the dead of winter. I always offered my assistance. It paid off for them. This job requires putting others' needs above your own.

In this line of work I have experienced personal satisfaction in knowing my efforts kept kids out of adulterous homes. Repeatedly unfaithful partners victimize children. Children get entangled between their parents because of an adulterous partner. Adultery affects their self-esteem. Adulterers verbally abuse and scar them for life. Children are forced into a new relationship with a non-biological parent. Courts have granted relief to my clients and their children. The court order prohibits a new boyfriend/girlfriend from participating in visitation. They are not allowed on the premises during custody visitation. When they do, and I prove it, consequences follow. When the spouse remarries this relief is cutoff. But in the short term it benefits the children.

In cases I've investigated involving children, this evidence helps them. It keeps children from being in a home where adultery has divided the marriage. This is a positive result and also beneficial for them. I hope to prevent this situation beforehand. To quote Ben Franklin, "A stitch in time saves nine." This wisdom can apply to adulterous marriages.

I've seen the results of adultery on children. Young boys grow up to hate their parents. Although they were headed for good times in sports or school, they dropped out of activities because of anger or revenge. They turned from wholesome activities to drugs and worthless pastimes. Soon they found the wrong kids and made friends. Young girls, who were not getting the attention they needed at home, often began looking for it in the wrong places. Adultery has very real and negative effects upon a home. Maybe this book will stop someone from entering a relationship headed for trouble.

As I write this book I am hoping adultery victims, on a grander scale, will benefit from my experience. In my practice, furnishing this information to clients is limited by my schedule. Therefore, this book allows me to share these insights with more people. The information and techniques in this book are exactly what have helped so many others in the past.

Ask yourself, "Have I consented or contributed to infidelity in my marriage?" If not, then don't feel guilty. Clearly you are a victim. Victims, by default, blame themselves. Maybe your spouse makes you feel less attractive or inferior somehow. Isn't that wrong anyway? You might be experiencing the effects of adultery.

I believe just about every victim of adultery is not to blame. Unless you have openly approved of your spouse committing adultery, why should you take responsibility for the consequences of it? We will discuss how unfaithful partners use trickery to emotionally hurt you. Now you can fight back, recognizing the warning signs before it's too late.

Unfortunately, victims of adultery often react with denial. Denial is normal. Yet, it complicates a victim's life and compounds the process of discovering the truth.

Getting clinical psychologists involved in the emotional struggles and conflict may prove beneficial. It is a traumatic time. Their counseling strategies will help you work through many emotional obstacles.

Women are quicker to understand when their marital relationship is in trouble. They intuitively perceive changes that signal a need to discover what is wrong.

ഇ)ൗ

I've always taken this job seriously and focused on helping victims. Witnessing adulterous relationships is never pleasant. Frequently clients don't know where to go for good advice. They ask family or friends what to do. In some situations, the victimization process can become dangerous. Without professional help, victims will experience difficulties that are beyond them. If the information in this book provides you with direction, insight or a resource, then I'm satisfied. My aim is to help you heal.

Before we get started, however, we need to define adultery. We turn to the *New Webster Encyclopedic Dictionary of the English Language*, published by Consolidated Book Publisher, who defines adultery as "violation of the marriage bed; sexual commerce by a married person with one who is not his or her wife or husband."

Also, in *Law of Domestic Relations* by Homer H. Clark, Jr., published by West Publishing Company (c)1968 Hornbook Series, states "The usual definition of adultery is the voluntary sexual intercourse of a married person with a person other than the offender's husband or wife." Further it addresses three possible questions of voluntary character of the act by stating;

In the first, when the wife is the victim of rape, she is clearly not guilty of adultery. The husband who commits rape upon a woman other than his wife is of course an adulterer. The second type of case has caused more difficulty. When one of the parties, generally the wife, is insane at the time of intercourse with someone other than her husband, most cases have held that she is not responsible and therefore this does not constitute adultery . . .

Finally, the third type of case holds that the adultery is not excused when the defendant was intoxicated at the time, since her condition of irresponsibility was caused by her own fault. (Homer H. Clark, Jr., p. 328)

Now we need to cover what legally constitutes adultery. The above-mentioned source states "Most of the cases on adultery are concerned with the problem of proof. As so many judges artlessly put it, there are seldom eyewitnesses to adultery. The rule has thus developed that it may be proved by circumstances which indicate a) the *opportunity* to commit adultery existed, and b) the *disposition or inclination* to commit it existed . . . frequent association with persons of the opposite sex at night and alone, improper familiarity, visits to hotels, or apartments with the paramour, and similar conduct."

PREFACE

"NOTHING IS MORE NOBLE, NOTHING MORE VENERABLE
THAN FIDELITY. FAITHFULNESS AND TRUTH ARE THE MOST SACRED
EXCELLENCES AND ENDOWMENTS OF THE HUMAN MIND."
CICERO

DEAR READER:

You may think you are alone in this crisis. I must inform you, based on my professional experience, the trauma of adultery is much more common than you think. Regardless of how you may have acted, you did not cause, and therefore could not have prevented, your spouse's affair. If you are a victim of adultery, I urge you to learn how to prevent more harm. In counseling it is therapeutic to write a letter. I recommend you do this immediately. Go ahead and pour out your soul on paper sharing all your experiences surrounding this calamity. You may even want to send this letter anonymously to our website as an e-mail or our post office box. Perhaps we will publish your story and help others like you.

Please understand that temptation and fantasies are normal. A marriage requires commitment to achieve continued fidelity. Openness about this issue will make the journey easier. Recognize that even if you are partly responsible for problems within your marriage, you are in no way responsible for your partner's choice to have an affair. Prevention of adultery is an unreasonable expectation when you are the only one striving for that goal.

There are three ways you get hurt. First, it hurts to be a victim who discovers an unfaithful spouse. Second, you experience self-recrimination believing you could have prevented it. Lastly, you suffer from mental conflict rationalizing that it's not happening to you. Unconsciously this tends to affect your self-esteem all the more. It's like having a spouse who drinks too much but denies there is a problem. Until you accept the reality, you will receive no resolution.

For those of you considering marriage, the information presented here is also for you. Choosing a spouse requires finding someone who has common interests—professional, emotional, spiritual and psychological. If you see any of the warning signs of adultery while still dating, overlooking them could mean disaster for you.

CHAPTER ONE

VULNERABLE RELATIONSHIPS

"NINE-TENTHS OF WISDOM CONSISTS IN BEING WISE IN TIME."
THEODORE ROOSEVELT

R ecently my parents celebrated fifty years of marriage. It was a testimony to me that long-term relationships are possible. Our family secretly orchestrated a surprise party. Without a doubt I experienced many wonderful memories to cherish as we honored them.

First and foremost I was proud of them. A marriage requires tremendous "give and take," friendship, admiration, love, and commitment. That's what their marriage perpetually says to me. This celebration gave me a renewed appreciation of and insight into the institution of marriage. I felt a sense of purpose and meaning. Their marriage was a major accomplishment that called for celebration! If critics could share their thoughts, they might say: "A great life's work!" "A milestone worth reaching!", "A major realization" or " re-markable high point!"

Making certain my parent's were surprised, we filled a social hall with family and a wonderful circle of friends. As I surveyed the guests, I realized a remarkable majority of their friends were also faithfully married as long—or longer—than my parents. My parents have acquaintances I truly respect and admire. Can we attribute their successful marriages to having been grounded in a different era? Possibly, yet that's only part of the answer. Collectively, their long-term marriages are proud legacies of their own creation—their heritage. Even in the face of trials, hardships, and health problems, they have remained together. These friends have honored their marriage vows. Thirty years from now I hope to find my friends still married. My purpose for telling you this is to instill the idea that marriage is good, necessary, and worth defending. Let's be clear about one thing—men and women were not meant to be alone.

ഇരു

We all want to know what makes certain marriages work. At the same time, we wonder why others fail. What exactly makes certain relationships vulnerable? What puts marriages at risk of infidelity? Why do scores of relationships fail while others seem to carry on just fine? No easy answer exists for this question. We can, however, look at various factors that present obstacles to successful marriages. A marriage can survive many temptations, yet those spouses who don't recognize certain dangerous pitfalls are more susceptible to adultery and risk that their marriages will end in divorce.

LEARNED BEHAVIORS

The psychological community has studied a theory called

"modeling" that helps explain why certain spouses are more like-ly to wander. In this research, newborn animals are taken away from their biological mothers and siblings directly after birth. The researchers then study the effects of this separation. They may then introduce "substitute" caregivers and record any progress or regression in terms of the young animal's behavior patterns.

The results are very telling. Ducklings, for example, will fol-low a football or similar object exchanged for their biological mother. With no link to a maternal parent, they will follow almost any object. While this research may seem cruel, it demon-strates how powerful an influence modeling has during this impressionable age.

In the same vein, a child's youthful and formative experi-ences guide him or her all the way through life toward either a positive or negative lifestyle. Life experiences are stored from an early age. Subsequently, behaviors and choices are influenced by previously learned behaviors or "modeling."

With humans, removing the mother or the father leaves children susceptible to a fragmented life. In fatherless homes, for example, long-term issues, primarily for daughters, are difficult to overcome. Seeking to fill this void, a daughter may turn to friv-olous relationships. Mothers who bear the responsibility of rais-ing children alone must cope with significant pressures. When children lack the support and nurturing of both parents, this "balanced model" is not available.

It's natural for children to replicate their parents' lifestyle, behaviors, and expressions. I'm sure you have seen such similari-ties—coined phrases and behaviors used by both the parents and the children.   It stands to reason, therefore, that children dis-cover love at home—what it is, how it is expressed, and what it means. However, what they learn about love can be confusing. Love, when conveyed unconditionally—no strings attached—will be modeled and genuine. Passing on this form of love within a family is the most valuable modeling parents can give their children.

Conversely, siblings who learn that love is given with conditions, or as a means of reciprocation for something else, get shortchanged. A modeling of divorce, shallow relationships, or conditional love demonstrates that love is only a means to an end. That being the case, children will often repeat in adulthood the patterns of love they learned in their childhood. They will repeat them over and over again in other relationships. On the contrary, parents who model values of trust, commitment, and forgiveness provide children with strong emotional foundations and a healthy sense of the true meaning of love. These children will also go on to express the kind of love they learn over and over again in their relationships

Let me ask this challenging question, "What kind of modeling did you experience as a child?" Did your parents model genuine love and behavior that promote lasting and healthy relationships? If so, it's likely that you will follow their example. If, on the other hand, your parents' marriage was characterized by heartbreak and disappointment, you are more likely to follow this example in your own life. If your parents' marriage failed due to dishonesty, deception, and infidelity, it may be hard for you to avoid these same patterns.

Does this mean you are doomed to repeat the negative modeling from your childhood? Not at all! The human will is remarkable. If you desire to do so, you can go on to create healthy, loving patterns in your own life. As long as you are aware of the influences at work in your life, you will be able to choose a better way.

All of us make choices everyday and are subject to both the rewards and consequences of those choices. Each day is filled with options, good and bad. We may decide to stay married, work through problems, and deal with our choices. We are free to make excuses and run from trouble or to remain faithful, even in the face of adversity. What have you learned to do? What will you choose to do?

DANGER HIGH VOLTAGE!

Is arguing wrong? Do you know of a married couple that never argued? It's human nature to disagree. Our differing viewpoints, ideas, and upbringing are unique   therefore we disagree. Let's face it, by design men and women are not the same physically, psychologically, emotionally, and experientially. Men are more focused externally, while women are more focused internally.   When something goes wrong, men are more likely to blame others, while women are more likely to blame themselves. When a relationship gets into trouble, a woman will get involved and seek help. She will talk through the problem with a therapist or with other women. Women find conversation and fellowship pleasurable, supportive and therapeutic.

On the other hand, men can be independent, often preferring to keep their thoughts and feelings to themselves. When a man is asked how his day was, he might say, "It was OK," and that's it, even if his day was far from OK. But this can leave his partner, who wants to connect, feeling left out in the cold. These two very different styles of communicating can be a source of misunderstandings, disappointment, and grief. If, however, couples can learn to understand, appreciate and work through these differences, those differences can be the foundation of a wonderfully complementary relationship. Each person's strength can bolster the others.

At what stage has a relationship gone utterly out of control? Infidelity is one extreme. So is physical abuse. Any physical abuse may call for an immediate separation and possible departure. No one should be used as a human punching bag. No one! When a spouse resorts to physical harm to either control a relationship or dominate the marriage by force, it's time to escape and regroup. In many cases of infidelity, I've seen people injured both physically and emotionally, some with fatal consequences. What should your first response to physical abuse be? By all means document the injuries–and then tell someone!

I'll share a story that dramatically illustrates this point. In this case, the wife married after "rebounding" from her first failed marriage. The relationship started with a few indications of aggression, but she did not see this predicament as the neon sign reading "Danger Ahead." The husband was short fused about everything. Things quickly turned violent. His treacherous acts made her existence a living hell. These events culminated in physical violence during a business trip they took together, where the husband made a serious miscalculation that fortunately cost him dearly.

While attending one of the seminars on the trip, he returned to the room and started an argument. The disagreement turned ugly. After choking his wife, he thrust her head in a toilet. While repeatedly flushing, he nearly drowned her. Throughout the entire ordeal he threatened to kill her. She survived by submitting to his demands. While having lunch with her friend the next day, she took off her sweater, forgetting her husband's threats of future violence if she revealed the bruises. It was too late. The marks of the traumatic ordeal were obvious. Without hesitation her friend consoled her. There are times when help comes at just the right moment — as it did for this spouse. The wife's friend encouraged her to fight back, and together they acted quickly to stop this man.

First they photographed each bruise. Thinking clearly, they formulated a survival plan for the trip home. When safely home, the wife stayed with her friend using a plausible alibi. Next, they turned to the authorities for help. After reporting the abuse to the police, they called my office. It takes quite a lot of courage to hire a private investigator under these circumstances. I realize that and try to bring a high degree of sensitivity to my work.

During the husband's next out-of-town business trip the tide changed. The wife cleaned out their bank account just as soon as he left. Then, we caught the husband in an affair with his boss during the trip. Waiting for him when he returned home was a police officer. The husband was immediately arrested for his deeds, evicted from my client's house — one she had owned before they married, and fired from his job. He lost his company car and was left homeless and impoverished. Both the adulterer and his paramour found themselves unemployed. Apparently the company did not tolerate infidelity in the workplace. In short order, the entire matter was settled. High-voltage relationships such as this one rank at the top of vulnerable relationships and often include infidelity.

THE RATIONALIZATION PRINCIPLE

During a recent radio interview the show's host told me about a caller who shared her thoughts about why cheating is acceptable. This caller made excuses for divorce and infidelity. The kids were older and off to college and the grass was greener on the other side. Noticeably she was rationalizing. When the host asked for my opinion, I responded with this analogy: "Let's say that I competed in a fishing contest and noticed that the guy next to me had hauled in the biggest catch of the day. Would it be acceptable for me to take it from him? After all, I started fishing hours before he arrived. After years of losing I just had to have a trophy fish. It was just his tough luck that I was bigger than him. So I wrestled his fish into my net! No problem, right?"

What's the difference? What's wrong with going after what you want?

For starters, consider the real victims of infidelity: the children, relatives, friends, employers, and neighbors. Sure, the cheater on the radio feels her choices are right because they satisfy her desires and needs. However, what about the other people in her life that are forced to accept her choices? Who really gets hurt? They all do! She knowingly leaves a path of destruction in her wake, and its those closest to her who contend with the fallout or clean up the wreckage.

Now consider the man who insists he is not cheating, not "technically" anyway. Though not yet divorced, he is separated, so he feels perfectly justified in starting a new relationship. But how can this man, or his new partner, enjoy any real trust in this relationship or themselves? This man is willing to jump quickly from one unfinished relationship to another. What's to keep him from doing the same thing to his new partner? And why should his new partner have any real confidence in or commitment to him? For both of them, disaster lurks right around the corner.

The people in these two examples have invoked what I call "The Law of Least Resistance." They are self-serving. Their philosophy is that, "If it feels good, do it!" Anyone who subscribes to this view is likely to become a repeat customer to family court. They blame others for all their problems. Their lack of accountability ensures a life riddled with mistakes and broken relationships. Essentially we need to understand that marriage is not convenient. It takes more than just having a great physical relationship, bank account, or upscale lifestyle. Life always brings tests and difficult times. It's how you handle them that are the real test of your character and commitment. It's the real testament to your love.

PERILOUS PORTFOLIO?

When the main feature of a marriage is financial, failure often results. Take, for example, Ralph and Toni:

Ralph divorced his first wife and then married Toni. She owned a small, comfortable house completely furnished. All Ralph had to do was add his personal belongings. What a great deal! Ralph might have shown his appreciation to Toni by investing in the estate over time. He didn't. Some twenty years later, Ralph still refuses to pay for upkeep. Ralph kept what he thought of as "his" money in separate checking and savings accounts. He contributed to half the groceries, utilities, and a few other obligations. Toni gave up fighting for more financial assistance. Ralph handled his finances in secrecy. Why? Toni let him. But this eventually laid the foundation for further secrecy and deceit.

Ralph loved golf and had a membership at a private country club. Toni never joined him. Without fail, every Saturday morning Ralph left the house early, returning again late at night. That was HIS time. He never invited Toni or suggested she take up an interest in the sport of club activities.

Ralph had one child from his former marriage. Toni had two boys. Ralph paid for his daughter's college education and

Toni paid for her boys. Adding to Ralph's good fortune he was given a company car, paid vacation time, a great salary, and fabulous perks. Although he made others think he was generous, when it came to helping anyone with a need or worthy causes, Ralph was the miser. He hoarded his money, turning down every opportunity to part with it. Even when Toni retired from her long-term job, she worked part time to continue to pay for the house. Ralph never even helped her buy a car. If she wanted a new one, she had to use her own savings.

ജОരെ

By now, Ralph sounds less like a husband and more like a nightmare roommate. Eventually Toni discovered Ralph's secret world. He was, in fact, funding another relationship. Toni found him out and then the courts adjusted Ralph's money management for him.

As a side note, it seems the person who spends all of his or her time concentrating on wealth hardly ever enjoys good relationships. This kind of person will starve a relationship to stash a little more money, or carry on a secret relationship. The person who deserves your "for better or worse" should be your best friend. That means you deserve someone who charitably shares in the bad times as well as in the bounty of life.

OCCUPATIONAL WASTELAND

Gainful employment is not a guarantee in life. At one time there was a Fortune 500 company that guaranteed lifetime job security as an incentive to its employees. Not today. Downsizing is now an accepted way of cutting budgets. Displaced casualties can experience tremendous stress. To cope, some individuals take advantage of their time off for illicit pursuits. A void in employment can also take its toll as one spouse leaves the other behind. Issues of self-worth, if not carefully guarded, can creep in and pollute an otherwise solid marriage.

The spouse whose job requires constant or excessive travel away from home is also vulnerable. Other factors, including sexual drive, physical appearance, and ego increase the risk of infidelity. But what if you or your spouse has no other way of making a living? Then constant communication, love, and affection are needed both at home and during these periods of separation. Try taking your spouse on trips with you. If that's not possible or practical, then stay in touch by phone or other means. Discuss your feelings. Be open about your concerns. Loneliness is one more culprit of vulnerable relationships. One writer shared her story with me about her personal loneliness.

℘℧

"I have been happily married for six years. My spouse is on active duty in the military. After September 11, 2001, my husband was sent overseas and has been there since. He has had several sets of orders since then. We have been together just twenty days this year. After eleven months of sadness and dealing with our children grieving... I did the unspeakable.... I didn't do it out of lust or anger...I did it out of loneliness... I have yet to tell my spouse and cause him the pain... I don't know if I should... It didn't change my love or devotion. It just made me miss him more. Almost like a new appreciation for him and our life.... I am not the cheating type and I do not believe in it. But i also never thought I would be so alone for so long....I gave all the signs of a hurting spouse long before i took this action... My spouse could not deal with my loneliness because of his current job - "SERVING HIS COUNTRY." Not that he drove me to it. It isn't his fault that i fell short of perfect... How do i get passed this ????????"

ഇറ

LOW SELF-ESTEEM

Notice the lower case "i" used repeatedly toward the end of her desperate letter? Does this suggest feelings of low self-esteem and guilt for her actions? Likewise, is she feeling sorrow and remorse for violating her husband's trust? I believe so. Her reaction is typical. This letter is also an accurate representation of how infidelity affects people. Her words are gripping. Her pain is real. She is suffering from a choice—one that she wishes she hadn't made.

Low self-esteem invades people's thoughts and aspirations. It's a powerfully negative force that can dictate one's life. Low self-esteem often emerges on a daily basis. It can begin in the formative years or creep in at any stage of life.

Low self-esteem also sets the stage for prince charming to come riding in on his white charger, possessing all the right words, flattery, and charm. He sweeps his victim off her feet with his smile and electrifying gaze. Seeking attention, affection, and approval, victims fall prey. Once again, low self-esteem sets infidelity in motion.

WHAT GOES ON BEHIND CLOSED DOORS?

A healthy sexual experience with your life mate is gratifying. Sex is a gift of mutual enjoyment. The spouse who is intimately faithful reaps a lifetime of true companionship. It stands to reason, then, that one of the fastest ways to end a marriage is to find sexual gratification with someone else. Without fail, when physical intimacy is shared outside the marital relationship, there's always trouble. Just one act of sexual infidelity can bring about guilt, shame, and remorse. Country music songwriters are notorious for lyrics depicting infidelity done in darkness and secrecy, they only endorse the danger.

In the movie, Unfaithful, actress Diane Lane rides a subway train home after an adulterous episode. During this ride she is overwhelmed with emotions. Guilt wins out! Adultery is glamorized in many stories, especially on the big screen. This is a great lie and misnomer. Adultery is not glamorous. It's painful, humiliating, and it creates problems for years to come. This movie concludes with an ambiguous ending. Does actor Richard Gere spend the rest of his life in hiding or in prison? We never know. Either way his life is shattered by infidelity.

TO FLEE OR NOT TO FLEE ...

Often the examples of bravery or leadership rise from a person who has learned to be responsible despite danger or personal harm. Clearly we witnessed immeasurable examples of incredible heroism during September 11, 2001. A fire fighter, rescuer, or police officer who puts his or her life on the line for others is undaunted by fear. Escaping the risk is never an option for a professional fire fighter, no matter what the cost. This is a true example of a person willing to do whatever it takes—regardless of the circumstances or outcome—possibly even losing his or her life.

Spouses who run when things heat up demonstrate just the opposite reaction. Wanting to play and not stay, they seek comfort and pleasure from another. Selfishness rules this person. They are faithful to no one and nothing except to themselves and their escape route. In reality, running from a crisis does not fix it, it just delays the outcome.

THE STRAY PUPPY DOG SYNDROME

I've found this syndrome to be more prevalent with females. Losing a dog is upsetting. Looking through lost and found ads with the hope of recovering a lost dog brings a torrent of anxiety. The nightmare is overwhelming. What may have happened was the dog was thought to be a stray and picked up by a kind, gentle person. Soon the stray becomes family and never returns home.

Just like the lost dog, a wandering, lost soul can work his way into the heart of a compassionate female. He shares his weaknesses and dilemmas of life. Often touched by his feelings, she draws him in to give him relief and comfort. Making room for him, she turns from listening and caring to a long-term commitment. Compelled to rescue him, she marries him. Difficulties surface if she ends her role as a mother figure. This union comes to an end as he strays again to the next kind stranger.

A ROCKY BEGINNING!

Does this next illustration sound foolish to you? Sorry to say, but this is another true episode from my case files.

A woman named Carol called me because she was looking for an investigator to check out her new boyfriend, Chris. She told us her marriage was one of "convenience" and that her husband didn't care anyway. She was desperate to find out what her boyfriend was up to Friday nights. His constant excuses for not wanting to get together alerted her. We found out that Chris was not just out with the guys, but seeing another woman. She continued dating him, hoping for the best.

Approximately one year passed and a man named Tom called to inquire about our services. He suspected his wife of cheating. He was married to the Carol named above. Astonishingly this true story went full circle: Carol cheated on Tom and her new boyfriend cheated on her. Tom got a divorce from Carol after hiring another investigator who caught her. Due to a conflict of interest we had told him that our work load was too full and turned him away. They did not have a marriage of convenience; Carol just used this lie to be unfaithful."

ഉറ

It's increasingly common to learn of a second marriage beginning while the first one still exists. In fact attorneys, at least in New York State, often tell their clients just as soon as the separation agreements are legally formalized, they can "go do their thing." So why is it surprising when infidelity occurs in a marriage initiated by infidelity?

$\mathcal{T}$HE MORE YOU KNOW

WE HAVE IT ALL?

Thriving financially and enjoying all the comforts of life demonstrate our next couple's exploits.

Vacationing in exotic places, weekending at the summer house, and changing vehicles each year were the norm for this couple. Unexpectedly for Sandra, Jerry's wife, this good fortune and envious relationship came to a screeching halt.

This marital wanderer fights subconscientious warnings and flirts with danger. For Jerry what develops as mere thoughts soon grows into reality. He ventures into a secret life and surrounds himself with the arms of another woman. In time Jerry realizes what a disastrous life he has chosen. Looking desperately for a safe path out of his problematic journey he finds none. He feels overwhelmed, discouraged by his deeds. Remorse and shame fill his every waking moment. Jerry's trapped.

Sensing her husband is in trouble, possibly ill; Sandra prompts him to talk. This is all it takes for Jerry to reveal the truth. He reveals every detail.

߀ఉ

What may seem like "having it all" often puts a relationship at risk of infidelity. It happens to scores of couples with means who forget what price will be required for their behavior. The price tag is beyond their wealth. Their road to recovery is long and burdensome. "Having it all" is a trapping that can lead to a bitter end.

߀ఉ

Relationships are active, not passive. Developing a wonderful marriage is very rewarding and an admirable life goal. Without a doubt, matrimony is the finest experience anyone can enjoy. Traveling this journey with your best friend cannot be measured in finances, houses, or vacations—just love.

Identifying those relationships vulnerable to infidelity makes it possible to avoid them. Discovering you are in a vulnerable relationship is not cause for alarm but for action.

If you can identify with any of the situations discussed in this chapter, it's time to consider the eight warning signs covered in the next chapter. After thirty years of investigation, these behaviors have surfaced in almost every assignment I've handled. Once you know them, you won't be blindsided in the future.

CHAPTER TWO
EIGHT SIGNS
OF ADULTERY

"WHEN SECRECY OR MYSTERY BEGINS, VICE OR
ROGUERY IS NOT FAR OFF."
SAMUEL JOHNSON

Candy visited my office late in the afternoon. She made the appointment when her husband would not be suspicious. Next she gave her boss the excuse her daughter had a doctor's appointment. Graciously, he let her go.

When I first met her, like so many others, Candy told me her story. A few things in their marriage did not seem right. I asked her for details to get background and decide how to proceed. She was very frustrated after suspecting her husband of cheating over the last year. Candy tried her best to figure out what he was up to but she failed. This is quite normal. He took their only car to work at night and gave her no way to follow him.

After spending about an hour with Candy she said something that raised my suspicions. Her husband Bob was not coming home right after his shift. He showed up at three, four and as late as five o'clock in the morning. To avoid the truth, Bob told Candy he was restless, drove around and fell asleep in his car. He was having problems at work and needed a way to blow them off.

Fortunately, Candy tracked these events. Bob routinely

stayed out late on Tuesday evenings. His shift ended at midnight so coming home anytime after 12:30 a.m. was not normal, especially when he stayed out until five in the morning. Candy was a very smart client. She gave Bob the impression that she bought his excuses.

After gathering this information, my plan was to follow him on Tuesday evenings when work let out. Armed with all of Bob's background, a recent photograph, a description of his car and where he parked, I set out for answers. I wanted evidence.

The first Tuesday evening surveillance failed when I lost Bob at a traffic light. However, on the next try I was determined to run this light if need be and anticipate better. Just like clockwork, Bob got out of work on time, went straight to his car and left the plant. I stayed with him as we passed the intersection that had foiled my surveillance the week before. I made all the rest of the traffic lights. (They are one of the investigator's worst enemies.)

After twenty minutes of surveillance, Bob was downtown. He turned down an alley and parked. The headlights went out but he stayed in the car. I had to park down the street and go on foot. This is always a risky part of surveillance. I needed to make a choice. Should I get out of the car to get a closer look and risk missing his departure? Or, do I stay in the car and wait him out?

Soon thereafter I saw the shadow of another person getting into his passenger seat. I ran back to my car and started up the engine. I witnessed Bob leave this alley behind a few commercial businesses. He headed straight for a restaurant uptown with a blond female in his car. It was at that point I made the right decision. Getting out of the car allowed me to see what he was doing. Otherwise I would have missed the evidence that later developed. Following too closely or too far away can jeopardize the investigation, but everything about this surveillance went my way that night.

They went inside for food while I waited outside the restaurant. We needed a few pictures and some video for court, so I obtained them. After they finished and paid the bill, Bob and this woman went to his car. Right away they engaged in sex. They seemed unaware of their surroundings while they got intimate in this cheap "motel room."

Whenever I take on these assignments there is pressure. It's not intentional. It just comes with the job. I need to help the client and document the proof as though each case were going to trial. Most of the time, I work alone and must be prepared with photographic equipment for each situation. Also, I must make quick decisions. The wrong one can cost the client her proof, and cost me money and credibility. Losing the opportunity of ever being successful in the case is also possible. Affairs happen for many reasons and often don't last more than a few months. They may just happen once, so being prepared and skilled enough to catch the moment is critical.

Bob started the car with his girlfriend back in the passenger seat. They returned to the alleyway, but this time I watched where she went. The building had a back door and that is where she entered. She had to get back in for her next performance. She was a stripper. Bob left the alley and drove home. His wife by now knew he was coming home and faked sleeping when he arrived. She played into the story for her own good. The next morning she visited the lawyer and began divorce proceedings.

Bob was telling the truth, to a degree. He was in his car, but not sleeping. Candy thanked me for helping her get the answers that she could not get for a year. It put closure on this long ordeal for her. I went on to the next assignment feeling satisfied that I had exposed the truth. This is a typical case but

each comes with something new about the players. I've found
that getting to the truth is not always easy and can be dangerous.

ഇൻരൂ

We will explore several more real life stories in order to learn
from their experiences. There are many decisions to make. The
facts play a very important role in the process. It's my job to help
you through this process to get answers, so let's get right to it!

I've studied and solved adultery cases since 1969. In most situations, cheaters do the same things. They frequently show predictable patterns of behavior and go to the same places.
Therefore, we can learn from them. I hope to empower you in
this respect. Like any criminal unfaithful partners must be identified by who, what, where, when, why and how. We will uncover their methods and tactics. We will see what they do, where
they go, who they partner with and just how to get proof.

In three decades, I've met with, spoken to and helped countless individuals concerned about infidelity. The client and I discuss his or her marital situation and determine whether there's
any basis for suspicion. There are other times when clients don't
suspect adultery but believe something is wrong. In many cases,
it is adultery and they are shocked once the proof is presented.

After these investigations are completed, we routinely
expose adultery. I obtain all the evidence needed to testify in a
domestic relations courtroom. I've always told clients that when
you have a toothache, you call the dentist. When you believe
your marriage is in trouble, you call me. For many, making that
call is not easy.

Meteorologists can predict trends and patterns. They also
study records of weather conditions as a tool for accurate predic-

tions. When they see darkening skies and cold air masses approaching a warm air system, they know a storm is brewing. Lightning strikes, rain pours and flooding conditions create havoc. They know they need to warn others. In this regard, I'll give you eight warning signs of adultery as a resource to deal with unfaithfulness in your marriage.

These signs are not mutually exclusive; all or none of them may surface. Keep in mind, a single indicator may not be cause for alarm. The mere presence of any of these signs is not proof positive. Nevertheless, humans are creatures of habit, good and bad. Signs are indicators and provide direction. They warn of danger and offer insight into the mind of an adulterer, and we can use them to our advantage.

Let me offer a word of caution right now. You must not reach an immediate conclusion after reading these signs. I address many other issues that you will also need to consider. There is much more information to cover. If you read this section only and close your mind to the remaining chapters, it would be a real mistake. Be careful to think through your situation before affecting your relationship.

Now, let's look at the signs that I will identify. Let's cover them one at a time, in detail.

1. Defensive Behavior
2. Changes in Affection and Sexual Activity
3. Financial Woes
4. Communication Problems
5. Unexplained Absences
6. Need to Be Alone
7. Pattern and Lifestyle Changes
8. Wardrobe Renovation

As I explain these signs, we can make the same analogy we made with predicting the weather. They warn of danger. Sometimes the thunder is distant or right in your own backyard. Regardless, we react to the conditions. It may require finding shelter from the storms of life.

Those of us who have conducted various lie detection exams, such as a polygraph or psychological stress evaluator, know when a pattern of deception surfaces. We are trained to study patterns showing truth or deception. Classic deception patterns are indicators which give an examiner the means to detect the truth about a person or situation. Using these indicators will give you the ability to detect the truth.

You need to understand the truth and act upon it.

DEFENSIVE BEHAVIOR

"ANGER BLOWS OUT THE LAMP OF THE MIND."
ROBERT GREEN INGERSOLL

Tom came home late from golf in the afternoon and put the clubs in the garage. After changing his shoes and hanging up his wet jacket, he entered the kitchen. He was disgusted with the round of golf he played. A few tough holes kept him from scoring in the seventies. He blamed it on the storm. His game left him the way it did every time wet weather rolled in.

Tom loved the sport but his wife was not at all interested. No matter what he tried, Sally took no interest in playing golf. He needed the recreation and hoped she might join him. They shared few common interests.

Today, something Sally did made Tom ask where she had been. He had noticed the wet tire tracks on the garage floor from her car. Her Volvo's engine seemed warm to the touch. Tom was curious because Sally told him she was staying home all day to do housework. When he saw her, Tom noticed the clothes Sally was wearing. He thought they seemed too fashionable for house cleaning. So Tom posed a simple question about where Sally had been. She flew off the handle.

This one question turned into a major blowup. Sally stormed out of the house and called late that night from her mother's. She was not coming back. Tom was very confused. "What did I do to deserve this?" he asked himself. Later he found out she had been sleeping with someone else. She left him permanently after a few months.

∞ʘѲ

Of all the signs I find, defensive behavior is the most common. Adulterers become overly sensitive, touchy or closed about their actions. Most cheaters don't even realize they exhibit this behavior. This telltale sign is hard for the adulterer to avoid. Unfaithful partners cannot resist being touchy and high-strung, especially when confronted by an angry or inquisitive spouse.

Psychological studies show that animals use several defense mechanisms when in danger. Some flee, others freeze, and others attack, and so on. These mechanisms enable them to ward off danger and escape their enemy. Adulterers, though not animals, react to defend themselves and avoid the truth.

Let me give examples of this kind of behavior. Have you asked questions like these? "Where have you been? Why are you home late from work again? Why was the passenger seat moved? You just got paid, why is there no money in the checkbook?

Where did it go? Why are you getting dressed up to buy milk?" Most likely your cheating spouse will hesitate, become resistant or argumentative. You can expect the reaction to fit the personality type.

Don't be surprised if he has a plausible answer. However, he may go on the attack, thus creating fear and prohibiting any more questions. He may be very convincing and throw you off guard, putting your challenges to rest. This may make you question your motives and doubt your suspicions. Actually, unfaithful partners are aiming for this reaction. They like to fool you into a sense of security and a false sense of trust. You again feel safe. Possibly you feel that you overreacted. After all, don't we all want a marriage built on trust? Who wants to believe their partner has been lying to them, especially if you suspect another person is involved?

Spouses need to observe how their partners handle themselves in moments when you challenge them. I will repeat this continually: Don't ask direct questions if your spouse becomes defensive with you.

Many adulterers get indignant and angry just because you ask a simple question. This reaction should set off your radar detector. Keep in mind, this behavior may become a pattern, not one isolated response. When they protect themselves against questions or challenges about their behavior, don't overlook it. You will find that conflicts escalate as the affair runs its course.

Difficult as it may seem, this is the time when you must stop asking questions about suspicious activities and events. You will not succeed with interrogating your spouse, because it requires professional experience and expertise. The more you push the issue, the less likely it is that you will find out what the adulterer is doing.

As a private investigator, I always suggest that our clients refrain from asking tough questions. Spousal confessions are rare, especially from the lips of an adulterer. Even the experts fail in this pursuit.

Consider how easily truth works. For example, I tell my spouse where I am going and why. Let's use a simple trip to the grocery store. I have no reason to deceive her. The trip only takes a few minutes. I return with the groceries we need for dinner. She looks at the receipt later and it confirms the store location and my purchases. Stamped on the bottom are the time and date verification. She notices my attitude and disposition have not changed when I return. I might tell her about the checkout kid who put the eggs in with the milk and how I told him off. (For his own good, of course.) From this trip, my spouse finds no excuses or indications that anything is amiss. If she checks the odometer on the car, it will match the distance to the grocery store and back home. This short example depicts a normal life experience.

Now compare this simple illustration with recent trips your spouse has made. Did he come home late and possibly flustered? Have you noticed other changes in appearance or attitude? Do you feel suspicious of his behavior? Does your spouse seem preoccupied? Does he make you feel out-of-place and anxious? Have you found physical evidence like different colored hair on clothing or in your vehicles, or the scent of perfume? If so, strive for the truth.

Unfaithful partners hedge, avoid the truth, and obscure details. Behavior of this kind will alert you. Does your spouse ask why you need to know where he has been . . . and so on? This behavior suggests trouble. Here's another point to ponder. When a story is too detailed, explained and unprompted, I recommend you note it. You can do some homework later, when the dust settles. Explanations that are explicit and drawn out should raise suspicion.

Defensive behavior is one of the most common tactics used to hide the truth. Most cheaters lack training in behavior responses of this nature. This is to your advantage. I call it a "classic behavior." It helps divert the truth and keeps distance from the accusers. Not only will a spouse feel this effect, but friends, family and others will experience this defensiveness.

Let me give you another example. During a theft investigation at a factory, we asked everyone we interrogated for names of co-workers they might suspect. As a rule, thieves will not volunteer anyone. They think that being reluctant will divert suspicions from them, but a trained investigator understands this is a red flag. Honest employees volunteer names of people they don't trust. Dishonest employees can't offer names, because one of them would be their own. They want to keep the circle open, fearing it will close in on them. It's humorous to investigators, because the perpetrator's name keeps surfacing. That is why we interrogate them last. They need to squirm. It weakens them into a confession. You see, the criminal mind becomes defensive. This signal is very common to trained professional investigators.

Adulterers operate in much the same way. They use this defensive tactic as a ploy. Even after thirty years, it still amazes me that unfaithful partners have not changed the way they handle themselves. This dishonesty causes unfaithful partners to turn the tables, making their victim feel responsible. They make spouses feel guilty for even asking any vital questions. Do these phrases sound familiar? "Why don't you trust me?" or "I'm tired of you accusing me of cheating!"

In this situation, guilt is transferred to victims. Victims react in many ways. They back off, begin to question themselves or avoid further confrontations. The truth never comes out. Some victims find the prospect of living alone so frightening that they will overlook many problems. This thinking gives cheaters more control. Therefore, it further complicates the marital relationship.

Do you realize guilt drives cheaters? It produces many kinds of behavior. They very carefully cover up each adulterous event before facing their spouse. They are mentally, and possibly emotionally, prepared to handle any direct questions. They always have an answer! This reaction may appear almost spontaneous. Yet, in reality, they have a response prepared. It is a game to them and similar to the game "monkey in the middle or cat and mouse." In this game someone in the middle of a circle tries to catch the ball as others toss it back and forth. For the person in the middle, it is exhausting.

Just looking for "lipstick on the collar" will throw you off. Let's continue looking at some other signs of adulterous behavior.

$\mathcal{T}$HE MORE YOU KNOW

CHANGES IN AFFECTION
AND SEXUAL ACTIVITY

"TALK NOT OF WASTED AFFECTION, AFFECTION NEVER WAS WASTED."
HENRY WADSWORTH LONGFELLOW

Besides defensive behavior, a change in sexual behavior is another major sign that can reveal adultery. Sexual intimacy gives expression to a marriage. Meeting each other's physical needs brings love and satisfaction. Consequently, sex is one key factor in a marriage that gives the adulterer away. The adulterer merely goes through the motions and does not try to satisfy his spouse any more. This can be offensive and obvious.

In most cases, clients notice a difference in sexual drive. Partners may have already noticed certain changes in the amount or type of intimacy that they exchange. They may discover a change in desire. This is similar to a radical change in eating habits. We cannot discount those legitimate explanations for the change. As marital partners see a pattern or variation with the sexual side of their relationship, it could or may be a sign of trouble.

For instance, intimacy might become less frequent. Your partner may display a desire for new techniques. This may suggest your spouse experimented, learning something new with someone else. Let's face it. We get to know our spouse intimately. This is a gift of marriage. Sexual activity is clearly an obvious sign. We know how to gratify our partner and what they need. Intimacy that markedly increases, decreases, or modifies enough to notice leads to suspicion. More than likely, it is an indication that the relationship needs attention. Are you able to discuss how you feel? Does your partner want to avoid the subject? Were you able to express your physical needs openly before but now struggle to talk about it?

Mark was always adventurous. He loved to climb mountains, ride trails and stay in shape. Cindy liked outdoor sports and this is how they met. Fifteen years later, Mark still rode his bike and was physically active. This was not possible for Cindy. Her mother had died and her aging father needed much of her time, not to mention the house and kids. She got stuck with all the chores and housekeeping. Mark never helped clean up or contributed in any way around the house. He had been spoiled in his childhood by a family who did not teach these basics.

Cindy noticed a change in Mark's behavior. They had always enjoyed their intimate moments. They had sex at least twice a week. What seemed like subtle change in Mark became apparent to her. He was not interested anymore. There were excuses or complaints about his job demands. They just drifted apart sexually, but she never made anything of it.

One day an anonymous note arrived in the mail. It made Cindy burst into tears right away. Fortunately the kids were in school. The writer revealed that Mark was having an affair with his secretary. This explained why he did not seem interested in her any more.

80Q3

In most marriages, partners establish a pattern of desire in their sexual lives according to their life cycles. Males may want to engage in sex every day or every other day. Normal sexual relations are usually without any deviation from the pattern. You need to consider age, stress factors, fatigue and so on, to help you evaluate your own situation. Physically, the male libido can slow or increase with age depending on an individual's personal situation and health. Any marked differences in sexual patterns should give reason for victims to investigate.

One client reported her husband was impotent. His impotence started a few years before my client and I met. They had not been intimate for that reason. She was unable to discuss her sexual needs with him. She stumbled upon a bottle of prescription medicine that addressed impotence. The label had his name on it. After further searching, she also found her husband was hiding this medicine around the house, in sheds or cars. What surprised her was they were not having sex anymore. She had believed it was no longer possible. When she found the medication, it tipped her off that her husband, once impotent, was using the drug, but not for her satisfaction. My investigation proved he was a deceiver.

We all want and need affection, that warmth and fondness we receive from friends. Our spouse can be our best friend. This attachment strengthens us personally. We feel secure and emotionally healthy. It is either there or it's not. When it leaves, a spouse notices. A simple hug brings many positive feelings. It suggests we love someone. All it takes is a thoughtful expression. When these kinds of expressions of affection are gone, it may be time to take notice.

THREE

FINANCIAL WOES

"MONEY OFTEN COSTS TOO MUCH."
RALPH WALDO EMERSON

"**Y**ou get a job and pay the bills!" demanded Larry. Selena fired back "Where's your paycheck going to? I'll bet you have someone else!" Sadly, Selena was right. Larry never admitted to it during this exchange, but silently left that night. He refused to give in or talk about it.

Selena found evidence of Larry's misdeeds right in the checkbook. She felt so stupid; it was there all along. Larry wrote checks that showed he was cheating. For years, he did all the books, paid the taxes and bills. Selena trusted him since she was not good with the money. They agreed he would handle it while she managed the other affairs of the home. Everything was going fine until one day, late notices turned up. Selena got them and never told Larry about them. After he left the house, she discovered a few credit card charge slips for suspicious purchases. He charged meals, flowers, lingerie, and gift items. She became suspicious and tracked them down to an overnight affair involving Larry and a young woman from the plant where he worked.

§0CR

Most affairs require funding. For that reason money will work like a thermometer. It gauges your spouse's actions and reasons for spending cash. Cash flow needs explanation, especially if you are suspicious.

Either one or both adulterous parties may spend money for sexual encounters. Yet, sometimes they just want to have the sexual act and romance is not in the picture. These are the "cheapskates." They usually drive somewhere like a riverbank or a dirt road to engage in sex.

Usually cheaters go to a bar for drinks. Next they take their partner to dinner, then to a motel. Adulterous locations vary. For the wealthy, it is unlimited. Nevertheless, one's means and lifestyle dictate where the cheaters will be found.

Some adulterous partners demand more. They might be blackmailing your spouse for things or special treatment. Therefore, track money carefully. It is very important to know where the money goes. They get new clothes, trips or a car. The adulterer buys things to please.

Adulterers can deplete funds quickly and cause financial hardship for victims. Check credit card and bank statements, including investment accounts, etc., to find out if money is missing. If you wait, it may be too late and you can become victimized financially! One client told us she checks their investment accounts every day. Her spouse does not make a move without her finding out quickly.

℅ↄℂ

Clients have found purchases of flowers, jewelry, hotel rooms, or meals on credit card statements. Some cheaters are not very careful. They leave a trail of unexplained purchases.

Amazingly, cheaters can be obvious when they know you have no control over how money is spent. Clients have found credit card receipts for dinners for two, dresses that wives did not receive and more obvious blunders. Hotel room fees appear right on their statements. It's possible to find expenditures on your account. Keep the proof. This shows inclination and possibly opportunity.

Look into all aspects of your finances to track down any evidence that your spouse is economically managing another relationship. Even if you cannot find any records, you can still learn how much money is missing and possibly when it was spent.

Are certain holidays, trips or vacations costing just a little bit too much? Is all the money accounted for? Are you seeing more debt or expenditures not related to your own spending?

COMMUNICATION PROBLEMS

"TWO CAN NOT FALL OUT IF ONE DOES NOT CHOOSE."
SPANISH PROVERB

Take the story of Jonathan and Margaret. They left the celebration early that day after making a scene in front of relatives. Jonathan wanted nothing to do with being there. He made it clear by his gestures and lack of conversation with family. Margaret was crushed. Her mother suspected something had been wrong with Jonathan's behavior for months. Margaret turned off any opportunity to hear what her mother was saying about him.

They had fought over the littlest things. An empty cereal box in the cupboard made Jonathan very angry. He demanded to know why she had not shopped for more food that week. Jonathan slammed doors and raced off to work in the mornings. He seemed ready to pick a fight for no reason. He was not the same, no matter how Margaret tried to see it that way. Jonathan just wanted to get away from her. This scene with family clinched it for Margaret. Her mother was right. There must be someone else.

&)(&

Poor communication surfaces as another major sign. Conversations with your spouse can change or become nonexistent. It may suggest a ploy to avoid answering for an adulterer's activity. What is your spouse really saying? Is there a real reason why things are rough? Do you know the root cause of your problems?

Various forms of conversation, if we can call it that, occur. Often adulterous partners verbally assault their victims. Maybe your spouse tells you to dress up more, put on more makeup or make changes in your personality. This may suggest a comparison with a partner. Will you hear "sweet talk" very often? It's doubtful. Is the romance gone?

When a partner is cheating, many conversations result in fights over little things. Communication problems in a marriage are not always an indicator. Yet, when we study communications it provides a great deal of information. We can see that something is wrong by our conversation.

Marriage is seldom without its disagreements, but most of the time cheaters live in a different world. Being able to manage two worlds successfully requires a real "con artist." Most cheaters are not that shrewd. Does your spouse appear to struggle with daily conversations? Look carefully as you attempt to converse. Often, criticism dominates the adulterer's mind and verbal exchanges with his spouse occur.

At some point you will find yourself becoming victimized. This is a direct result of adultery entering the marital home. Adulterers transfer their guilt subconsciously. They have to sustain an appearance of a loving relationship. This guilt causes them to justify their actions. Eventually they upset the home. Cheaters also pick verbal fights just to leave the home. It is a trick to get them where they want to go.

If you suspect that conversations are failing because of an affair, you must avoid asking direct questions. You must be prepared to investigate without being discovered by your spouse. It's like tipping off criminals just before they commit their next crime. They have time to cover up any evidence and thus gain a real advantage over you. Adulterers quickly make up needed stories and excuses, and you lose at this point.

I am referring to what I call "hot button" questions. Avoid questions about specifics. Don't ask for the name of the suspected partner, the place your spouse went last night, times and events, the address of the partner or her husband's name. Giving up the short-term satisfaction is better so that you can document the whole story. Stay away from these areas. Our goal is to get the truth, but trying shortcuts like those never works.

UNEXPLAINED ABSENCES

"ALL DECEPTION IN THE COURSE OF LIFE IS INDEED NOTHING
ELSE BUT A LIE REDUCED TO PRACTICE, AND FALSEHOOD PASSING
FROM WORDS INTO THINGS."
ROBERT SOUTH

"**W**hat's wrong? I'll tell you what's wrong!" Benny shouted on his way out the door. "You looked at me the wrong way again. You buy off brand foods and you need a new hairdo, that's what!"

Off he went, not letting Mary know when to expect him back. He behaved the same way two weekends in a row. He would call from Dan's late Friday night and say he not coming home until after the football game on Sunday.

Mary could not call Dan's place because Dan was Benny's brother. He would cover for him and always did. They used to get in bar fights together, and being twins, they watched each other's backs so well they avoided getting caught many times. Mary knew Dan would lie for Benny this time, too. Lying became a pattern for them when in a pinch. They gave each other alibis, so it was no use trying to call. Danny was a liar and a creep. Mary had to let it go. She had no car and no one to call for help. Her family lived on the east coast. Maybe she made a mistake marrying Dan, but she had been pregnant. It had been the only way.

§ロ03

Jim's story was a little different. He argued with his wife Judy about small things but he never dreamed they would divorce. Judy had made an issue of Jim's one time search of the Internet for a pornography website. She never let it go, making it the reason for a divorce. Jim was stunned that even after he had admitted wrongdoing to Judy, she had never forgiven him. It seemed odd to him that she would make his life miserable over this one thing.

He worked on a retail vending route for years. His wife, Judy, worked at a local retail store. They had no children. His day started much earlier than Judy's. Their schedules crossed paths in the evenings. Jim carried a cell phone for business and became suspicious when, on several occasions, he phoned home before Judy was supposed to have left for work, and the answering machine came on. Jim did not want to accuse Judy without being sure of his suspicions.

I placed Judy under surveillance before she got out of work. Jim would get home earlier than she and saw a pattern. Judy came home much later than her shift change warranted. I watched Judy get in her car and drive off from the store parking lot. She was not going in the direction of home so I made sure to stay with her. In front of a two-story apartment house Judy parked her SUV. She went upstairs and turned on lights. I could see her silhouette through the windows. Within minutes another car showed up and parked in front. She had a male visitor spend the night.

The next day, Jim and I met as planned. When I shared the news, Jim was devastated. All along he had never suspected Judy of seeing someone else. It was not like her. Her parents were happily married. She came from a good home. Jim even knew the partner when I showed him the pictures and video. He worked at the same store as Judy.

Jim and Judy parted ways, yet Judy had a big surprise coming. She had been caught in adultery and it changed the case. Jim's attorney spelled out the details of her affair in his divorce papers. Judy settled out of court within two weeks. She did not want to be embarrassed in court by my testimony. I also knew she did not want her lover subpoenaed to testify. Not only was he her boss, he was married.

ᔕᗝᑕᖇ

Has your spouse been missing often? Is work keeping him away from home? Has he no excuse for his behavior? I usually find that cheaters cannot explain their actions well. They don't show up when they are supposed to. They miss quality time with family. It starts with the occasional "I forgot, sorry." Then the absences evolve into everyday.

Besides being away from family, cheaters have a problem with time management. On one or more occasions, they'll get sloppy. Noticeable time goes by and they are not home when they should be. They can't make appointments or show up as expected. It becomes a problem for the adulterer.

In some situations, cheaters use their work time to commit adultery without being discovered. Do they really go into work at all? Are they calling in sick or taking personal time to rendezvous? So often, adulterers come home late when it does not make sense.

Some are not that good at preparing a story and come up with lame excuses. Remember, we are trying to catch the cheaters red-handed, not get a confession. So accept any excuse for the time being. Hunting is never easy. It takes patience, determination and skill. My approach is no different.

Adulterers must manage time during their affairs. You can be sure time becomes their enemy. When you suspect something is wrong, meticulously track their time. Knowing how long it takes your spouse to get back and forth from work and other places is valuable information. We will cover this later.

Take the information suspected adulterers provide and use it for comparison or analysis later. Consider further investigation if where they tell you they were would have been impossible.

When your spouse is spending too much time at the same place, you should be wary.

THE NEED TO BE ALONE

"ALL HUMAN ACTIVITY IS PROMPTED BY DESIRE."
BERTRAND RUSSELL

Eddie loved the outdoors. He was part of a wildlife group whose mission included preservation activities. He never missed its weekly meetings. His interest in this group's mission and purpose just seemed unnecessary to his wife, Joan.

She suspected Eddie of being unfaithful for many reasons. I agreed to get evidence if he was using these meetings as an excuse. After a few meetings, Eddie's behavior seemed fine. He went straight home each night.

Joan let me know that Eddie rarely came home so early. He usually lingered at least an hour or more. It was not like him to come home so soon. It was about three weeks into the investigation that Eddie told Joan he had to get away. He was going camping in Canada for two weeks. No one else was going, just Eddie. He made that clear. All he wanted to do was be alone for a while.

Using my knowledge from past investigations, I showed up the morning Eddie's flight departed. He drove his minivan to the long-term parking area, removed his luggage and headed to check in. Joan suspected a member of the preservation society and gave me her photograph. Since the weather was very cold, my van windows were difficult to keep clean. It interfered with the job of watching arriving passengers. Car after car arrived during the hour leading up to his departure time. One of the vehicles that dropped passengers was a cab. There, in my binoculars, was this female from the photograph. She entered the check-in alone and played it cool. It was shortly after she got in line that the two of them embraced.

Two weeks later they returned from Canada together. They were on the same flight, from the same city and at the same time. What added to the evidence was the fact that this flight was delayed at an airport in the Midwest due to snow. It was scheduled to arrive at the original time. When they both got off this flight together, the chances of them being together coincidentally were unlikely. They were together intentionally.

While Eddie was in Canada, he phoned his wife at home. Prior to this call, Joan had no means of contacting him. He never gave her a hotel phone number or itinerary, attempting to avoid detection. Of course, we helped lay this trap. Following my instructions, Joan refrained from any inquisitiveness. She never asked Eddie about his trip, and he never volunteered any information. As expected, Eddie's actions were predictable. When given this freedom of choice he reacted as do most adulterers.

Joan called Eddie two times during his trip for different reasons. In the background she heard another voice, that of a female. The second time a female answered the call and my client hung up. This is like hunting; you try not to disturb the niche. After this couple left for home, I obtained a copy of his hotel bill, which showed there had been two occupants in his room.

ഇറ

Does your spouse make plans without you? Cheaters want to leave the house, alone. They make excuses to find a way out. They may be very clever or obvious, depending on their personality and upbringing. Are they taking vacations alone? It's common to hear clients say that they never suspected anything was wrong with their spouse having to take a trip alone.

Cheaters find ways to be alone. They might have a "midlife" excuse. For instance, you might hear him say, "I need time to sort things out" or "I'm so stressed out, I need to get away for a while."

Some cruel cheaters have led their spouses to believe they were suicidal or depressed as a way to manipulate their situation. They might leave a note suggesting they were going through a major life crisis. Yet in reality, they were violating trust. This is a very painful deception. You can imagine the feelings of betrayal that come from this act.

How frequently does your spouse want to be alone and away from home? Does this pattern of behavior make you wonder if it has merit? Ask yourself whether your spouse has a good reason for this behavior. Of course, marital partners sometimes do need to be alone. They need to build relationships with others but not to the extent that it causes problems with a marriage.

In a marriage, we cannot or should not be together every

waking moment. Staying married under that arrangement is not possible. Adults need time to socialize or engage in normal activities without their spouses. But spouses who use excuses to get out of the house create suspicion.

SEVEN
PATTERN AND LIFESTYLE CHANGES

"THINGS DO NOT CHANGE, WE DO."
HENRY DAVID THOREAU

Robert's life seemed rather boring. He got up without an alarm clock, exactly at 5:00 a.m. every day. His routine was making the coffee, read the paper, shower and go off to work. Precisely at 5:15 p.m., his wife, Peg heard the garage door open and Robert climbed the stairs to the kitchen. With a peck on the cheek, Robert changed and then relaxed in the family room until dinner.

His weekends were spent cutting the lawn, washing cars, gardening, and then he rested. A late night for Robert was 9:00 p.m. He rarely needed anything fancy and everything had its place. His life was very neat and organized. Robert was credited with the finest-kept home and cars on the block. He was envied.

After turning 40 years old, Robert started slipping out of his routines. The sound of the garage door opening got later each week. A few times he would remember to call, but Peg told Robert it was fine that he was late. She could reheat the food when he got home. Eventually, Robert's routines changed. Now he was never on time, his interest in the house and garden was gone. Weeds dominated that section of the yard. They were an eyesore, so Peg tilled the garden over and threw seeds down. She had to pay a neighbor boy to cut the lawn. What had happened to her Robert?

⁗⁗

Ted never liked sports. His friends tried to get him interested in sailing. Getting Ted to sail, fly, ski or bowl was never possible. For years, his wife Carla wanted them to try something together. She finally gave up.

Ten years after they were married, Ted started a new job. He seemed to change during the first year working for the stock brokerage firm. Ted was not the same person. His normal appearance had been casual. Even during ceremonies or funerals, Ted had worn the same clothing.

Carla witnessed, as the months passed, changes in Ted's appearance and interests. The changes were dramatic and left an impression on Carla. Not only was he dressed better, he was now interested in those activities she had always wanted to do. The problem was, she was not included in Ted's plans. There was always an excuse. It wasn't long before Ted was found with a fellow employee from the firm. Carla got a call from a high school friend who saw them bowling together. Carla was embarrassed and made an excuse for Ted. She said it was a friend of the family and she could not go that night. The whole situation made her sick.

⁗⁗

"Why do we need that car? You already have a nice van!" questioned Sandy. "I just want it!" said Toby. "We can do just fine with the one we have," added Sandy. "I want to look younger!" said Toby. "You're an old man. What do you need with a BMW?" Sandy returned.

ಬಂ

Any lifestyle change will be noticeable. As this change emerges, spouses will encounter a new fixation. However, it's when this is contrary to their nature that it is most obvious. The lazy man does not like to exercise. A sluggard hates any work. Their actions become suspicious.

Dramatic changes have a reason. If you have no clues for them, probe for answers to these patterns and lifestyle changes. Has your spouse been on a diet? Does he bring home items that have nothing to do with you, like a new-found hobby or interest? Is your spouse taking up tennis or racquetball? Is he all of a sudden "preppy?" Have these noticeable changes made you feel left out? Do you see this "new person" surfacing for no good reason?

This metamorphosis could have an explanation. One client would always know her husband was cheating by the way he dressed up. He had never used cologne for business events before, but suddenly made it a regular practice. He had also hated attending them before. Now he was sure to go to all of them, even leaving early to get there. This was out of character and signaled trouble. Another thing to ask yourself is why your spouse has not asked you to join him.

Look for patterns taking form in your spouse. For instance, every Tuesday night is golf with the league. Maybe for years your spouse really did golf and came home on time. He was never late!

Nevertheless, now he's late all the time. As suspicions rise, patterns may confirm you have a problem.

Cheaters reinforce patterns if never challenged or placed in check. Rest assured your spouse is monitoring your every move. He will be ready when you push "hot" buttons. Watch as you close in, either intentionally or by accident. If you mention anything about this change, your spouse becomes defensive. Adulterers are always on alert. Like a good hunter, don't distract them.

With each pattern, you discover more information about the affair. Psychologically, the adulterer knows he is engaged in wrongful behavior. Cheaters cannot escape these feelings of guilt. It motivates behavior.

Unfaithful partners may want to buy new cars to make them feel young or more physically appealing. They will argue over which type of car they need. Taking the station wagon is out of the question. They need the coupe. Can you hear an alarm going off? It may only be a subtle signal, but it is one that you cannot overlook.

The Hamilton and Smith families were best of friends. Their children were the same ages. They partied together, enjoyed vacations together and the wives confided in each other. The couples dreamed of traveling the world in their golden years. They had ideal marriages.

As women often do, Mary recognized a change in her friend John's outward appearance. Even more disturbing to Mary was his behavior. Mary really got along with John's wife Amy but did not feel comfortable about discussing her observations. Mary surmised John was suffering from a life threatening illness. Needless to say, she was troubled but too afraid to bring up the subject in conversation.

Within in a few weeks Amy called Mary, upset, and wanted to talk. Mary fell apart when she learned John left Amy for
someone else. Not only was Mary grieved with the troubling
news but it affected her way of thinking concerning her own
marriage. Over time Mary grew to trust her marital relationship. She did recover from this surprise, but not without considerable anxiety. It made her re-evaluate her own marriage.
For some time after this shock, Mary found herself giving into
things her husband wanted just to keep him happy. She
responded in a different way then she usually did, not realizing
she was trying to avoid a collapse of her own marriage. Mary's
overcompensation for her feelings of insecurity finally passed
with time.

EIGHT
WARDROBE RENOVATION

> "ALL CHANGE IS NOT GROWTH; ALL MOVEMENT
> IS NOT FORWARD."
> **ELLEN GLASGOW**

Ken would never wear certain clothing styles. Every
Christmas his mother sent him the latest fashion of pants,
shirts, jackets and ties. He packed them away and complained
about her choices. His selection was more conservative. Helen
heard him say "this stuff is too flashy" but she really liked them
on him. Size was not the issue for Ken, just the look. He was
very satisfied with his wardrobe. Helen thought he was very
bland but gave up any hope of changing Ken's appearance.
After fifteen years of marriage Helen suspected something

was wrong. One of the dead giveaways for her was Ken's attire. He pulled out the Christmas gifts then shopped for new clothes. He bought tighter fitting pants, new jackets and took on a flashier image. Helen asked him why. Ken made light of it and moved on.

"Have you seen Ken lately?" Jennifer said to Kim. "Yeah, he's a real hunk," Kim said. "What's up with him? He's married. Does his wife Helen let him out dressed that way?" Kim and Jennifer's conversation was overheard by a mutual friend of the family who relayed the discussion to Helen. This made her feel awful. Her husband was making it obvious he was trying to get girls to notice him. His appearance made it quite apparent he was available. Ken also took off his wedding band.

∞CR

Are you noticing any new suits, dresses, ties, or shoes in the closet? It's possibly an indicator. Cheaters also buy sexy underwear despite the drawers full of plain ones that were fine for years. Have thongs become part of the wardrobe? Are new teddies hidden away?

When you think your spouse is going out without you, check the attire. When they leave the house, quickly search clothing drawers. Take inventory of missing garments. One astute client knew when her spouse cheated by the underwear he wore that day. Given her watchful eye she noticed he wore a certain pair when things seemed suspicious. She also checked to see if he came home with the same pair on.

This leads to another consideration. After most sexual encounters, evidence is possibly left on garments. You should make it a priority to inspect the clothing in question secretly and thoroughly, especially underwear. Look for evidence of pubic hair or signs of sexual activity. Is the hair different from yours or your spouse's color? Smells are clearly an indication of an affair. Store the underwear in a brown paper bag. Labs can test these garments for fluids. DNA tests are affordable and conclusive.

If cheaters know their clothing needs washing, they will attempt to do it quickly. We have known adulterers to immediately wash clothes when they came home. Others just bring a change of clothing and wash it later at a laundromat.

Clothing can tell you if the adulterer has been around animals. This would be significant if you don't have any pets. Here's another thing to consider; you may have dogs but the clothing smells of cat urine. Your partner may have entered a home with the smell of other animals. They may have sat on furniture that left a smell. You may find traces of human or animal hair, lipstick or food particles, so search for them.

When your spouse first comes home, immediately try to embrace. See if your marital partner rejects your advances. Be aware of perfume or cologne scents. They may suggest something after a disappearance. If your partner came home late one night, check the clothes. If you have a dog, watch if it reacts to smells on your spouse's attire. Your animal may create an awkward situation if your spouse just had a rendezvous.

Another aspect of clothing worth investigating is inconsistent dress. Be suspicious when your partner's clothing is inappropriate for certain appointments or events. If the situation calls for casual dress and your spouse goes out in formal wear, it does not add up. It is not normal. Why? Where are they really going? What if it is a change for them to get dressed at all? Naturally, any flirtatious dress will raise questions in your mind.

Does your spouse remove the wedding band? Keep in mind that due to some professional or medical conditions, removing this ring is necessary. Still, I suggest this is an action worth challenging, at least in your own mind. Wearing a wedding band is a symbol of your heart. It is not merely a legal gesture. It's a token of love and commitment. Wearing a wedding band reflects a complete circle. It says there is no room for others.

CHAPTER THREE

WHERE IT ALL BEGINS

"YOU CAN FOOL SOME OF THE PEOPLE ALL THE TIME,
AND ALL OF THE PEOPLE SOME OF THE TIME,
BUT YOU CANNOT FOOL ALL OF THE PEOPLE ALL THE TIME."
ABRAHAM LINCOLN

A major accomplishment for you is determining the identity of the adulterous partner. Some clients have already discovered this piece of the puzzle and just want proof. Consider these suggestions in identifying the adulterous partner.

Assuming your spouse still lives with you in the marital home, we can detect many things. However, if your spouse has moved out, you have a greater challenge. Also, a spouse not living at home creates a shortage of information for your investigator. Clients no longer have access to current patterns, behaviors, and attitudes. They cannot monitor the events of the day. If your spouse has already moved on, your investigator will need to conduct surveillance during nights; weekends or events that you believe are suspicious.

It's time to look at the most likely places where adultery is occurs. We will start with the most prevalent places and continue from there. Explaining every site is not possible because humans are too creative. Each area is totally different and leads to other possibilities. Using these suggested locations will help you evaluate your own situation.

ON THE JOB

The workplace is the most prevalent place where adultery is cultivated. There are many reasons why this is true. The main reason is that most adults spend considerable time there. They have frequent contact with others. With this daily activity, adultery gets fostered. Your spouse may find someone attractive and you would not find out. Of course, this depends on their ability to keep their actions secret. Frequently a secretary, boss or co-worker is the partner. The opportunities are greater and easier during working hours.

Depending on the type of employment, victims should consider names of people of the opposite sex that they mention routinely. For now, begin registering names of employees who come up in conversations. You may be further along in this process, so consider names from the past as well.

One client reported that his wife held lengthy conversations with her boss when she came home. They called each other daily and did not appear to talk shop. Then suddenly his name never surfaced again. Eventually, after I was hired, I caught them at a local hotel together.

THE BAR SCENE

Cheaters frequent bars to find partners. It might happen just once or become more progressive. Does your spouse need to stop for a drink after a sporting event, or stop at the bar on the way home from work?

Does he play in a league where they celebrate after games? Did your relationship start in a bar? It's very common to hear from a client that when their spouses frequent bars, they experience trouble.

Don't forget hotel lounges where your spouse spends time during business trips. Also, gentlemen's clubs attract many customers. Is your spouse a regular guest?

On The Net

With the arrival of the Internet and our ability to reach out to the world, spouses have reported their partners visiting the Web to cheat. Ironically the name "web" connotes something a spider uses to catch and devour its prey. I've seen the Web destroy many marriages. Spouses consumed by the Internet are likely to find sex websites and chatrooms where they connect sexually with other consenting adults.

Does your spouse spend too much time there? Does he quickly turn the screen off when you enter the room? Are passwords hidden from you? Is he spending countless hours in chatrooms? This is another breeding ground. The web is full of lustful places. You should care what is being done on the internet. Clients frequently report their spouses have started relationships via Chatrooms. Partners may surface from your area or your spouse may travel considerable distances to have an encounter. I am finding unusual circumstances due to the internet.

Prior to the evolution of electronic security software, I developed a computer routine to catch email and chatroom conversations for clients. My software routine provides volumes of data without a spouse's knowledge. Software companies have since developed even more sophisticated versions which are a much needed help in our mission. These software packages are designed to capture all keystrokes, visited websites, and chatroom conversations in addition to storing images of each website in a retrievable record. Users of such software can review all internet activity on any computer it is installed on. Such software is an important surveillance tool and is available from our website.

To further assist my clients in the evidence collection process, I offer a forensic search to retrieve deleted files, images, and records of internet use. This is a very effective tool in combating infidelity. When a spouse believes that files were deleted from a family computer there is hope. We can recover this information as a service to our clients. It's possible that deleted or hidden files may be recovered by our forensic search. Our report reflects the nature of all discovered text files and pictures previously stored on that computer. This service is often invaluable not only in cases of adultery but is useful in the detection of other crimes like embezzlement, drugs, terrorism, fraud and sex crimes.

Most internet software programs provide an audit trail when they are used. A record is stored when a site is logged onto or even searched. Checking the "History" and "Search" functions of the software will give you details of computer activity. You should print any such activity to protect it from loss.

SPORTS ENTHUSIASTS

A sports hobby provides the venue for extramarital relationships. This common ground is the opportunity to meet under a legitimate cover. Sports are healthy physically, mentally and emotionally. Anyone enjoying healthy pursuits is normal. But I've seen the onset of adultery when two people took their children to the same karate classes. Adulterers can use this love of sports to cover up their tracks.

HEALTH CLUBS

Does your spouse frequent the gym alone? It's an obvious place to see barely dressed bodies. This is a place where macho men look for sexy girls. They work out and possibly become attracted to someone they see. It may be a gradual thing that leads to a relationship. Suspect health clubs as places to find adulterous behavior. For that matter, any club memberships are opportunities to find an adulterous partner.

PROFESSIONAL SERVICES

Is your spouse receiving counseling with anyone? Is he meeting regularly for other forms of professional services: the massage therapist, golf or tennis instructor? I've seen adultery occur when partners share personal and confidential information with them. They might be vulnerable for some reason. Professionals can take advantage of this situation. Opportunists find weakness and seize the moment.

Don't overlook an adulterous partner in the professional realm. I am referring to counselors, advisors, psychiatrists, psychologists, teachers, clergy, etc. Perhaps your spouse is undergoing regular care at a health provider. It affords an opportunity for them to leave the house with an excuse.

Your Neighbors

Obviously, adultery occurs in many environments, including your own neighborhood. Have you noticed any flirts in your neighborhood? Don't overlook them. This means you must look at those who reside in the same development or have regular association with your family. This would include acquaintances from the school your children attend.

If you enjoy the use of a community hall, or condominium association building, keep a watchful eye at these locations. Any common meeting place or facility where you use services, like laundry, swimming or games, are target sites.

Old Flames and Ex-spouses

Has someone come back into the picture? Has your spouse been spending too much time with a former spouse? Are the children's visitations going too well? Maybe your spouse insists upon flying back to an old hometown for overnight business? Evaluate your circumstances to spot a chance of an old flame reigniting. Maybe he recently moved nearby and you did not know it.

Places of Worship

Routinely we find adultery in churches. Nationally, this problem has gotten much press. It is shameful but a reality. Clergy should never be left alone with a member of the opposite sex for any reason, especially in counseling. They should leave the door open or ajar. Smart ministers record their conversations or put a video camera in the office that others monitor outside. They don't broadcast any sound, just their activities.

Temptation, coupled with opportunity, increases the likelihood of adultery. Ministers, evangelists, priests, lay ministers, rabbis, and other religious leaders who claim to live a holy life, but have a mistress on the side, are only fooling themselves.

Often, married churchgoers look for opportunities to meet others. Places of worship are not immune to adultery. It serves as a cover for their activities. Not everyone attends church for spiritual reasons.

Does your spouse seem too familiar with a clergyman or church member? Clergy have a sense of authority, and in situations like this, may use that authority for sexual gratification. Unfortunately, I have personally witnessed clergy destroying churches and marriages by their covetousness, self-interest, and deceit.

Another important tendency that I've witnessed with regard to religious people is this: in the religious mind it is taboo to be divorced. This presents a problem for those who want out of a marriage and yet remain under the "law of God." In such case, spouses can try several tactics. They may use psychological warfare. Their goal is to inflict enough emotional and mental turmoil that their spouse feels like they are "going crazy." At times they may even suggest counseling for all the distressful comments made by them. Also, clients have reported their spouses try to put them in physical harm, hoping to end their lives. For instance, a spouse may try to accidentally drop an electric appliance like a hair dryer into the tub while they are bathing. This way, if they were deceased, God, their family and the religious community, would not be displeased with them if they remarried. It is a cruel person who does or even considers these things.

PORNOGRAPHY

If your spouse is turning to pornography, being concerned is legitimate. When books, magazines, or sales literature turn up in your home or spouse's possession, it can suggest trouble. Are you aware of your spouse frequenting adult bookstores? Has he tried to engage you in such activities? You may even check with your local video stores to see how many adult videos he has rented. I am suggesting this activity often contributes to infidelity. However, it would be unfair to state that all pornographic activity leads to an affair.

THE OTHER PROFESSIONALS

Regular companionship with a prostitute has no excuse. Frequenting a house of prostitution or visiting with a prostitute is hard evidence of adultery. For a spouse to associate with prostitutes means the marriage is in trouble. When a spouse turns to prostitutes, they also will have other symptoms, such as alcoholism, drugs, involvement in pornography and so on. This is a very serious state of affairs for the victim. The marriage may also suffer from violence. Professional counseling is recommended.

CHAPTER FOUR

DO THEY RENDEZVOUS?

"DON'T PLACE TOO MUCH CONFIDENCE IN THE MAN
WHO BOASTS OF BEING AS HONEST AS THE DAY IS
LONG. WAIT UNTIL YOU MEET HIM AT NIGHT."
ROBERT C. EDWARDS

The call came late in the afternoon when I was planning to close for the day. A client just learned his wife was going out Saturday morning. She would not be back all day. Carey drove a van and liked to go shopping alone. She routinely took off for groceries but the trips seemed to take quite a long time. Matt started to suspect their marriage was in trouble. He was so convinced by Carey's behavior that he retained my services. We arranged to follow Carey. Matt was briefed to call me when he suspected a problem. When we finished our meeting, Matt left and I expected to start surveillance for him in a few weeks. Matt called within two days. I freed up my schedule.

As planned, I got in position near the entrance to Matt's development. Carey had to pass that way to get out. The arrangement was that Matt would call when she left the house so I could see her leave the neighborhood. It was not a location where I could sit near their house and watch. Despite what viewers see on television, real investigators must be creative and less conspicuous.

I was ready with cameras and a cell phone. It was about eleven in the morning when he called me. In a hurried first conversation, Matt just wanted to know I was there. After this assurance he had to wait until she left the house to make the next call.

Some twenty minutes later, Carey got in the van and Matt raced to the phone again. He told me to expect her any minute. In my rear view mirror the dark green Caravan was in sight. She was alone and in a hurry. Racing to the main highway, Carey passed several cars. Her alleged agenda included shopping at a local bookstore, but why was she in such a hurry?

Within a few minutes Carey drove toward the section of the mall where the bookstore was found. I could not get through the light and was stuck waiting for the traffic to cross. This was frustrating. "She got me!" flashed across my mind. When the light changed, the cars in front of me seemed to take their time, adding to my anxiety level. I found her van parked in front of this crowded store. She was not in the van. "Now what do I do?" I thought. "Do I go inside the store, or wait outside for her to leave? Carey will probably buy a book to get a receipt, then go about her business from here."

After searching the store I turned up nothing. She was not inside. I went right to my van in time to see something that would make my day. I lifted my video camera to capture the image of Carey getting out of her lover's car, taking an overnight bag from her van, then returning to his car. They sped off with me behind them. I got a real break when Carey had forgotten to take her overnight bag out of her van the first time.

That Saturday was a very busy day for shoppers and it was a real challenge to stay with them. Red light after red light, I was one or two car lengths back. Changing lanes occasionally to throw them off seemed to work. When I pulled up next to this couple, they were obliviously headed for a day of pleasure. Following the highway, they went straight to the interstate. I was still behind them with cameras rolling.

Up came exit four. "Are they getting off here? That's good!" This section of town was filled with hotels. "Could they be going right to one?" I asked myself. "This will be too easy. They don't usually do it this way." Most of the time I have to spend hours following people before they commit adultery. To my surprise, they passed the first hotel, and then turned around in a parking lot right after it. It was at this point I thought they "made me." This is a phrase that in my business means that I got caught spying.

Driving past them was my only choice, but I lost view of their car. Quickly I circled back through the neighborhood and found a place to see them park in front of a hotel. They had not seen me. This job was quite easy from that point on. Now I just needed to wait for them to leave. For most of the day it rained very hard.

Matt called a few times during the day out of curiosity. He was the type that needed reassurance that everything was going right for him. Many clients want to offer advice or like to challenge my methods. It's normal. My clients are going through this experience for the first time.

Carey made a call home to Matt sometime around 8:00 p.m. She told him she was not ready to come home, but was going to the movies with some friends; she would not say with whom. The movie she chose was on cable. This way she could tell Matt about the movie she had watched.

Later that night around eleven Carey and her lover returned to the bookstore. I had to race back there ahead of them to capture more video. Taking a different route paid off for me. I got in place with my camera to watch them arrive.

Carey got out of the van and her partner was very affectionate. He loaded flowers and a suitcase into the back of her van. They openly embraced and kissed. I focused on their wet hair, hair that was combed differently from earlier, suggesting a shower. Since they were not exposed to the rain after entering the hotel, I would point this out on video. Also, the hotel had no pool to explain this discovery and evidence.

This guy was someone Carey had met at a local music studio. Her son was taking lessons with his daughter. The relationship was suspected but not confirmed until my investigation.

ဆာင

Glenn was a police officer. He earned many awards for his bravery and duty to service. With his extensive training and special talents, being away from family for police work seemed normal. Unexpected calls from the station beckoned him from home at various hours. His wife, Mary, was very proud of Glenn. She made a lovely home, prepared him meals and really took care of him when he was home. Mary was industrious around the house. She painted, wallpapered and fixed up their dream home while Glenn worked.

It was not surprising when Glenn would dress in his uniform, and leave the house right after holiday meals for work. Glenn worked every Thanksgiving and Christmas evening shift.

After a few years, Glenn was discovered to have another family. It was no wonder he had left early during the holidays and weekends. He was not working but keeping another relationship. This secret life continued undetected for several years. Eventually he disappeared without notice and was later found in the arms of another woman. His years as a police officer helped him to cover his tracks. Another factor that fostered this relationship was a very trusting wife and family. He used his call to duty as a ploy each holiday to dress in uniform and leave for an unexpected assignment. All along he was maintaining another relationship. It turned out that he had another family the whole time.

ഇൗരു

Obviously, predicting a rendezvous is nearly impossible. Nevertheless, my experience shows that they occur at many locations with regularity. The following times or events are suggestions for monitoring the cheaters:

WHEN DO YOU LOOK?

Weekends/Evenings

Weekends and evenings are routinely when investigators conduct surveillance. Most affairs involve activities during this time. Most bars have happy hours or special activities that bring couples together. Adulterers disappear more systematically on weekends. I spend Friday and Saturday nights placing subjects under surveillance. This is when parties happen, social events occur and cheaters try to get free.

Lunches

Employees' lunch hours are routine surveillance assignments for me. They have this time off legitimately. The self-employed person's schedule is more liberal, but lunch is a good hour to observe them. It's possible to disappear long enough for an encounter. Co-workers can make appointments with the doctor or use some other excuse just to meet your spouse. It's common for people to have long lunches. Taking two hours during the day will rarely cause anyone to think twice.

Days Off

Your spouse and a co-worker can take the same days off to rendezvous. If you work and are busy when your spouse is off work, then consider this time as prime time. Employers often have no clue their employers are using the workplace to facilitate adultery. A simple phone call to the supervisor with a legitimate excuse gives them a means of seeing each other. A spouse may learn from someone inside the workplace of this activity, but most people do not want to get involved. Anyone who has received help from a source on the job can consider themselves to be very fortunate. In this situation be certain to protect your source from any backlash.

Before and after Work

Cheaters leave earlier for work than scheduled. Let's say work starts at eight a.m. daily. If your spouse increasingly leaves home at six a.m. you should be suspicious. I've heard clients tell me their spouses used the excuse that they needed to get in earlier to cover for someone or get an early start on a project. They may use the excuse of wanting to please the boss. This may be legitimate, if they have always been an early riser. To the contrary, a spouse who does not want to get up early has another real purpose that you need to explore.

Arriving home very late from work should raise suspicions. Cheaters make up excuses about new plans or projects that require them to leave home earlier. They may tell you that the boss needs them to stay late. This pursuit coupled with the other signs will tip you off.

Birthdays of Partners

If you suspect your spouse is cheating with someone you know, find out when he or she was born. It's a good day to place your spouse under surveillance. Check to see how your spouse dresses, the day's plans, or any other unusual activities on this date.

WHERE ARE THEY FOUND?

The Workplace

Without question, this is the first place to look. Partners' relationships traditionally develop in the daily work environment. Cheaters have all day to make contacts, use the phone, send E-mail, stop by the cubicle or have lunch together. All these activities have the appearance of work. If adultery is not affecting the adulterer's employability, the relationship will continue.

Sometimes sexual harassment plays into this mix. I've witnessed bosses using their position for sexual intimidation.

Remember, I've been in this business before laws made this illegal. Once I caught a boss using his position with a temporary employee at a hotel. He told her to cooperate as a means to a better job. She did. This case resulted in a lawsuit, and the boss ultimately lost his job.

Business Trips, Conventions or Out-of-Town Assignments

Business trips are a real part of executives' careers. Meetings out of town are normal. Conventions are held frequently for various businesses which can include travel to almost anywhere. They are great places to check out suspected cheaters. I place them under surveillance during their morning activities on departure days. If they go to the airport, I watch with whom they speak and board the aircraft. I'm not surprised when they pick up a partner for the trip. It's also smart to see them return. Sometimes they may take the partner home.

Anyone who has a job where travel is involved has opportunity. Executives, sales or service professionals are most likely to have free time. Self-employed spouses have the freedom to cover their tracks. They are also very difficult to catch, even with professional help.

Sporting Trips or Events

Sports outings, like hunting or fishing trips, and trips to health clubs, concerts or stores allow time out. A spouse may take their lover along during these events, especially trips out of town. Watch for airline tickets, charges for hotel rooms, or extra supplies on credit card bills.

One client, whose husband was a funeral director, took his partner out of state on a business trip. They stayed in a motel together, and then returned home with a silent witness in the back of the hearse.

Shopping

Spouses will use shopping to leave the house undetected. They will usually bring clothes home from a store where they shopped. However, the time supposedly spent in the store was excessive and when asked about it, their attitude is very cold. All the signs are obvious as to where they really went.

Schooling

If your spouse attends college or another form of education or training, consider checking out this time away from home. Watch their schedule, and then monitor arrival times after classes. Are they really studying at the library? Their grades will reflect it.

CHAPTER FIVE

GET THE PROOF!

"TRUTH IS MORE IMPORTANT THAN THE FACTS."
FRANK LLOYD WRIGHT

We will assume that you have done everything right so far. You have not tipped off your spouse, made threatening phone calls to the suspected partner, called everyone in the family about your suspicions, and so on. This chapter lays out many aspects of conducting a successful adultery investigation. Each aspect is necessary, yet not all of them are possible. Pieces of the puzzle will fit into place as you work diligently. When you do one thing at a time, it can and will amount to considerable evidence.

Evidence can be both tangible and circumstantial. You will need witnesses, photographs, video, documents, reports, receipts, letters, and events to prove your case. If you just want to satisfy your need to know, your tasks will not need this intensity. In this position, you are the judge. How much proof you need is up to you. However, this will not be the case if you go to court!

Circumstantial evidence is normally easier to obtain and prove in contrast to direct evidence. Often circumstanial evidence is an observation. We can reach inferences while not possible with direct evidence. Meanwhile, investigators frequently win court cases by what they have observed, heard, or experienced while investigating these types of assignments.

I suggest you put feelings and emotions aside. This is easy for an independent observer but you may struggle if you are a victim. Conducting your own investigation may affect you directly or someone near to you, making objectivity that much harder. An objective witness has a clearer insight into the truth. You must keep an open mind, not one clouded by hasty conclusions.

The definition of adultery we mentioned during the introduction guides each investigation. Proving inclination, intent and opportunity is necessary. We must document any outward signs of affection either on film or video. Witnesses are helpful with other evidence. You must prove there was opportunity for a sexual encounter. Usually it happens at night and in a place where others are not present. The easiest place is a hotel or apartment. Each situation differs but I've testified to the simplest of circumstances as well as some really complex ones.

For example, one couple met at the spouse's residence. He owned a very large mansion in a highly rural setting. The house was set back off the road several hundred feet. Foliage surrounded the property and trees lined the driveway. The closest house was some distance away. Ferreting out a place to watch this house was nearly impossible. My only option was sitting about a half-mile away from the driveway. It was a very demanding assignment. Later that night, a state trooper checked me out because I was easy to spot.

I had the client's permission to go on the property to verify that both their vehicles were there. After completing that portion of the task I headed back on foot to my vehicle. As fate would have it, someone came down the driveway and I had to hide. Running was in order. I found that hiding behind one of those large trees lining the driveway worked. Fortunately, they did not discover me. What is so memorable is the small pond that I did not know was on the other side of this hiding place I selected. I was very thankful to have stopped just short of taking a splash and getting caught. As it turned out, the next morning I met in a hotel conference room with two lawyers. The lawyer for the wealthy spouse grilled me for facts, and then turned to the other lawyer wanting to settle this case. This settlement came quickly. I had never experienced such a fast resolution before. As part of their agreement, they required that I maintain the strictest confidentiality of the identities of these two parties. Their names were well known. Adultery was a dangerous game in that state and era. The stakes were high. News coverage of the event would have created devastation, so settling out of court was the answer. My client was pleased with the swift negotiations. They paid me and the story is one that I've shared for years. Of course, I've kept my promise to hide their identities.

℘)℘

Now it's your turn to get the proof. Nevertheless, beware of jumping to conclusions. A premature judgment leads to falsehoods. Reaching hasty decisions is also costly.

In this chapter there are several steps to help you find the truth. We expose the darkness by turning on the spotlight. We need facts to do this. Let's see how.

STEP 1 • THE HOMESTEAD

Many places can be searched to gather evidence but the first place to start is at home. It is perfectly normal for you to feel uncomfortable about this. As a victim, your life changes from composed to hysterical. Learn to go along keeping an open mind. Consider the following ideas in your quest for the truth.

Diary

The first order of business is to buy a diary which you keep secretly. Start recording conversations, details, and events on a daily basis. This information will also help you and your attorney prepare for court later on, especially if you have forgotten exact details. Memories often get clouded by time and emotions. Don't trust that you will have the story straight. The best way to remember events is to write them down.

Date each page, noting times each event occurred. Describe where you were, what happened, why and if any witnesses were there. Collect information on incidents or activities as they develop. Look around the house, office and cars for phone numbers, addresses, places and activities to record.

Record details of conversations you had with your spouse, suspicious events, mileage, behavior and information to help you piece the puzzle together later.

Within several months, dates and times will run together before you realize it. Some of us have difficulty recalling things. That is an excellent reason to put it in writing. Also, diaries are important to your testimony before a family court judge. Notes you take when things happen are a great source of truth. Your testimony will come across as believable. When you are sticking to the facts, it conveys the issues better. Keeping a written record is also a way of comparing information you learned from the various sources I suggested in this book. This record is important. Don't forget to hide it!

Trash

You may not believe it but all too often a treasure trove of information can be found by sifting through the trash. Armed with gloves, begin searching your trash. Look for papers, letters, and envelopes with return addresses, company stationary, logos and details to help your discovery process. Don't be surprised to find pay dirt in your receptacles. I have cashed in on many trash ventures. Just when you don't feel like checking, do it! This one activity can provide more information than several others combined. Use it to your advantage. Remember to be secretive. Why lose this option just because of carelessness?

Laundry

Habitually search your laundry for clothing your spouse wears. Search pockets for information and clues of an affair. Inspect the clothing for any evidence of smell, soils and changes indicative of foul play. Don't be surprised if your spouse tries to keep you from certain pieces of clothing. He may even panic when he finds you doing the laundry.

$\mathcal{T}$HE MORE YOU KNOW

Bank Statements

Monthly statements provide a history of purchases and usage. You have a record of dates, locations and dollar amounts to scrutinize. This information helps you track any patterns or suspicious activities. Besides normal house, car and living expenses, your bank statement shows where your money went. Record any cash advances in your diary. It will start making sense if a pattern develops. Maybe a certain holiday, date, day or event will surface. Make photocopies of these monthly statements without your spouse knowing.

Get copies of cancelled checks if needed. Ask the bank to send them to you. Later, I will address your need to rent a post office box. Request that the bank send the copies there. For security reasons, many banks will not mail cancelled checks but will allow you to pick them up. If they will not mail them go to the bank. By obtaining these checks, your local branch will be giving you valuable information that your spouse may not be aware of.

Study dates and amounts carefully to track down where the paycheck went. You may find useful information. Has your spouse wanted a separate bank account? Why? When did this start? Exploring this funding is important but stay away from tipping your hand.

Credit Cards

How well do you track your receipts? Be meticulous with respect to all charge accounts. Analyze all of your monthly statements, checking to see if any month's statement is missing. Call the company and ask for the missing statement(s).

Find out if your spouse has a separate charge account. Get copies of those bills. I've seen clients bring in copies of charges that clearly indict their spouses of cheating. When a hotel charge appears for unexplained dates, you can use it as a basis for a challenge in court. Records of purchases for personal items can explain where your spouse has been and what he or she has done. Little things like flowers, candy, clothes and perfume divulge information.

Bedrooms

Savvy clients have made their beds a specific way in an effort to find information. They know right away that someone has used the bed. Check the carpets for shoe prints. Vacuum the floors on purpose before you leave to identify any changes. Place items around to tell you what changed or moved. Folding toilet paper on one corner shows its usage.

Hairbrushes

As strange as it sounds, we have seen lovers leave behind traces of their hair in hairbrushes. They use a brush or comb either in the victim's home, car, office or elsewhere that clearly provides evidence. Traces of hair can be very noticeable. This is especially true when your family members all have blonde hair and you find a red hair strand. Consider the hair strands for color, length or type, i.e., straight or curly. Let me again raise caution about tipping your hand on this subject. Never make it an issue before considering your overall course of action.

Should you save the hair strand(s)? Yes. Place findings in an envelope, plastic sandwich bag or brown paper bag along with an index card reflecting the day, date, time and location it was discovered. Seal the envelope so you don't lose the contents. Using hair strands as evidence is very unlikely, but you may need to convince someone, such as a lawyer, of your suspicions. It improves your position and possibly adds to the proof.

The most important part of this discovery is to make certain the hair follicle is not from a family member. It might also come from someone you let into your home legitimately. This can include relatives, guests or friends you had in your home or cars. We may rule out any suspicion immediately when a match from these people follows a recent party or event where they would have used your hair brushes. A good suggestion is to clean your brushes and combs as you go through this period of time.

This may be a fine point, but we may know our brush or comb was used by tracking movement or new activity. Unfortunately, clients have reported their personal utensils were part of the adulterous affairs. It sickens them. However, the important thing to bear in mind is that when the brush is isolated from personal access and a new hair type is on the bristles, we need to investigate why.

Take this piece of evidence and compile it along with other suggestions we make to reach your conclusion.

Showering

While your spouse is showering, take this time to check things out. Search wallets, purses, briefcases, gym bags, etc., for names, phone numbers, business cards, receipts, letters, matchbooks, photographs and so on.

One client found rolls of film her spouse took during a European business trip. When developed, our client had evidence of the affair. The pictures clearly identified the partner. Several photographs showed her provocatively dressed and posing seductively on a hotel bed. The noose tightened further when this travel companion posed in front of the Eiffel Tower. Guess where her spouse conducted business that trip?

Amusingly, this client allowed her cheating husband to search frantically for the film. While he was busy, my client slipped out to a local film developer and in one hour had color prints. When she returned, he was still in a frenzy scouring the garage where she had stumbled upon the film.

Condoms

If you use them, keep an accurate count. The depletion of condoms from the bathroom closet has been an important clue clients have found. This started them on a road to discovering their marriage was in trouble.

Sleeping

Searching when the adulterer is sleeping is also possible and may be necessary. Only you know when and where to search so be careful but take the chance. If successful, you must immediately take evidence to a safe place. Use a bank safe deposit box or your lawyer.

You can probably copy a love letter or picture and put it

back. This evidence may just be the straw that breaks the camel's back. Don't lose it. Clients repeatedly win negotiations with just a little more evidence in their favor.

Eye Contact

Consciously look directly into your spouse's eyes when you converse. The eyes are the windows to their soul. During many lie detection examinations, liars appear powerless to make direct eye contact. While questioned directly, adulterers will also find it hard to make eye contact. You might see them look away or lower their head. This is body language. Looking your cheating mate square in the eye will challenge the deception. This will not be used in court, but may add circumstantially to the proof you need to convince yourself.

STEP 2 • LINES OF COMMUNICATION

The Phone System

Take the time to review your phone bills. If your spouse is self-employed, check those business phone bills as well. Cellular phone calls can reveal information that you must not overlook. Some phone companies allow you to get a copy of the bills sent to a post office box. They will also send you an itemization of local calls separate from your regular phone bill. This way they do not tip your spouse off.

Contact your phone company and request itemized bills that include local calls. They call this feature "local accountability." You may have to pay extra for this service but it is normally a good method of learning whom your spouse calls. Get this portion of your bill sent to a post office box separate from your spouse. However, this will not work if your name is not on the billing.

Hang-up calls are not always wrong numbers. They can be messages. Frequently partners are directed to hang up, revealing to adulterers that they are free to meet. Adulterers commonly make calls just before going out. They may also receive a signal at a designated time.

Regularly pressing the redial button is a helpful technique. Be ready to record the redialed number. This will require a tape recorder and connecting cabling. Investigators can decode the dialed number.

Calls that are not traceable might originate from a cellular caller, payphone, bloked ID caller, or calling card user. This is valuable information. Some telephone companies display the identification as "Out of Area." This is OK because it's another lead. Ask yourself why your spouse is receiving them. It's not the whole answer but a start. You will at least know that communications are under way requiring your attention.

If the redialed number is not residential but commercial, it may still be informative. For instance, it could be a hotel, restaurant, business, or other location. This may tell you where they meet. It might show the partner's employer or a business near their residence. This phone information becomes a part of your file and, in time, may prove useful.

Another tip is to use automated features offered by most phone companies. For example, pressing *57 in some systems just after a suspicious call, places a record on your phone bill. This feature records the date, time and caller ID on your bill each time. The phone company charges a nominal fee per usage. By using this feature, another piece of valuable direct evidence may be collected. It works if someone is harassing you over the phone. Annoyance bureaus at phone companies use the technique to verify the harassment.

In some telephone systems, pressing *69 will provide the identity of the last caller. This can be done if you do not have Caller ID. Jot the number down in your diary.

When your spouse uses a cell phone, do the same things. Press "redial" for the last number on the phone. Check and copy the bills. Analyze them for details about phone activity and contacts.

Telephone Accountant

With technology today, you can take matters into your own hands. An apparatus called a "telephone accountant" has the capacity to monitor up to twelve hundred outbound calls. It registers and prints a log of numbers called, plus the date, time and length of calls made from your phone. It is a great idea in difficult cases.

It is possible to find out phone customer information. It's actually very simple to do using directory assistance websites.

Calling Cards

See if your spouse is using calling cards. Finding out who they called is not possible but might suggest more spousal deception. Used cards may turn up in your trash. You may also find them in a wallet or purse.

Friends

Routinely, adulterers use friends, willing or otherwise, to aid in their adulterous activities. They might go so far as to ask friends to cover for them. Try calling your spouse's friend when the spouse says he will be there, but you suspect he is not. Don't let on that you suspect anything. Find a reason to call first and make it easy to appear you foolishly called. Ask to speak with your spouse and see what happens. You might even record this conversation. Replaying the information later may be useful to you.

Recording Devices

In some states it is a felony to record personal conversations, even in the privacy of your own home or vehicle. New York State, for example, requires that at least one party participates in the conversation and is aware of the recordings. Lawmakers call this law "one-party consent."

If permitted by law, record telephone calls in the car, home or office. This will not only "cut to the chase" but quickly give you the verification you need.

WARNING: Do not depend on this information alone to prove your case. It is merely a means to an end. Most courts will not accept this evidence and you will need to meet rules of evidence to satisfy a court as to authenticity of the recording. Leave this task to the experts.

You can install recording devices anywhere on the phone line. A feature called VOX (voice activated) on the recorder automatically starts and stops recording while the phone is in use.

There are twelve states that require "all party" consent; California, Connecticut, Delaware, Florida, Illinois, Maryland, Massachusetts, Michigan, Montana, New Hampshire, Pennsylvania and Washington. Both parties involved in the conversation must give consent to have their communications recorded in these states.

The remaining thirty eight states are referred to as "one party" consent which include; Alaska, Arkansas, Colorado, District of Columbia, Georgia, Hawaii, Idaho, Indiana, Iowa, Kansas, Kentucky, Louisiana, Maine, Minnesota, Mississippi, Missouri, Nebraska, Nevada, New Jersey, New Mexico, New York, North Carolina, North Dakota, Ohio, Oklahoma, Oregon,

Rhode Island, South Carolina, South Dakota, Tennessee, Texas, Utah, Vermont, Virginia, West Virginia, Wisconsin and Wyoming.

Two very useful websites for researching current laws on wiretapping are:

http://uscode.house.gov/usc.htm
> This is a government website with a searchable database of the "United States Code."

http://www.rcfp.org/taping/
> The second is sponsored by "The Reporters Committee for Freedom of the Press" offering an easy and clear description of individual state laws on wiretapping. They post "A Practical Guide to Taping Phone Calls and In-Person Conversations in the 50 States and D.C."
> (This is a sight worth visiting.)

If you are so inclined the federal statues applicable to wiretapping are:

TITLE 18. CRIMES AND CRIMINAL PROCEDURE,

PART I—CRIMES and CHAPTER 119 "WIRE AND ELECTRONIC COMMUNICATIONS INTERCEPTION AND INTERCEPTION OF ORAL COMMUNICATIONS."

The United States Code website mentioned above has this entire legislation. Here's the webpage:

http://uscode.house.gov/uscode-cgi/fastweb.exe?search

Again, you must know and obey the laws in your state before recording any conversations.

STEP 3 • High Tech Stuff

Hidden Cameras

Miniature cameras today come disguised so well that you can videotape affairs at home or work. Investigators or specialty security shops sell them. I rent or sell these cameras to suit my clients' needs.

Technology now allows clients to install hidden cameras in a matter of minutes. You can plug systems today into a wall outlet and get immediate video images. Cameras are moveable from room to room. These devices can pay off.

A quality industrial VCR recorder is necessary. I use motion detectors that trigger the recorder when activity occurs. It eliminates hours of reviewing nothing. Also, videotapes don't run out that way. This single feature reduces wasted time and frustration.

I install cameras in many locations and let the equipment do all the work. We can install and dial up cameras via phone lines. A computer, coupled with a few peripherals can view the inside of your house, office or apartment, from anywhere in the world. A skilled technician can hide a camera almost anywhere. I have hidden them in pagers, purses, ties, hats, wall pictures, lamps and more.

Wireless systems can be set up in less time. Clients see no extra wires other than the usual power cord for a household table lamp or clock radio. This also permits the movement of a covert camera to various locations as needed. The only drawback is the distance you can move the camera from the receiver unit and VCR before signal loss. Most wireless systems work within one hundred feet or more. Interference of the video signal is possible. In most houses these systems work very well. We do not recommend exposing this type of equipment to extreme cold, heat or water. Placing them in or near these elements will cause damage.

It's also possible to install a miniature camera system inside of a vehicle. You can record to an 8mm VCR (a miniature video recording unit) or even transmit video evidence. A surveillance vehicle within range receives video images. Entire units can be placed under car seats or in trunks. You must regularly change the tapes and possibly the batteries. Monitoring these tapes can determine where the adulterer went each day. You may have footage of hotel locations and much more. Partners may be in plain view or their house may be identified from the footage. It is only another tool and not for everyone but is invaluable under the right circumstances.

Jim hired me to install a covert camera system in his house. He suspected Sarah of cheating. They worked for the same company but at different locations and shifts. Sarah worked days and Jim nights. Sarah was not affectionate for months. They never resolved fights and she acted very defensively.

I found this project very difficult. They had a small house, which created limited options for the equipment to be installed without detection. We used a wireless clock radio that he put on his side of the bed. Jim was ready to explain his reason for spending the money for the new clock radio. Sarah was still nasty about him spending the money or why he needed his own alarm clock. She was always petty. Jim handled himself well and she let it go. I found the attic to be a great location for the rest of the equipment. The video recorder, wireless receiver and video monitor were hidden behind several boxes. I needed to cover the long extension cord that ran across the flooring with more boxes.

Next, Jim was shown how to operate this recorder and change tapes. After a few days we met to exchange the used tapes for new ones. I reviewed them but found no evidence. Jim got discouraged after two weeks of this operation. I convinced him not to give up and finally Sarah was caught with an employee from work in her own bedroom. This ended her lies and Jim ended the marriage.

❧◉❧

This type of case is often the exception, in my experience. Rarely do adulterers use their own homes for affairs. However this real example shows just how foolish people can be.

Vehicle Tracking Systems

Vehicle tracking systems store information to reveal exact street locations every minute of the day for up to a month. Tracking software is used to download vehicle activity and document where the adulterer traveled. Tracking systems can be very useful. You will need to find an investigator familiar with this new technology. The receiver is placed in the investigator's vehicle. We attach the transmitter to the subject's vehicle signaling its location.

This is different from a Global Positioning System (G.P.S.). A G.P.S. obtains vehicle locations from satellite systems interpreting their signals. Antennas must have a clear path in order for the satellite to track them. Your investigator will provide you with a report containing daily routes your spouse drove. You will have valuable facts including dates, times, and locations to review.

Difficult assignments require creative solutions. Some assignments make it necessary to track vehicles electronically. Check with your local investigator.

Handwriting Analysis

Graphology is the science of interpreting personality characteristics through handwritten text. The use of expert handwriting analysis can be very valuable in some circumstances. Studying relationships between handwriting traits and respective character traits is useful. When a love letter surfaces, a graphologist can study it for personality traits. When they analyze a document, they can verify the signature as authentic or a forgery. For example, you may need this service if you are dealing with a forged signature on a tax form. Your investigation can prove it was not your handwriting. I have used experts to detect the type of personality behind anonymous and threatening letters.

Perhaps your spouse left a love letter around and you found it. Analysis and comparison for court purposes can show you confirmed the new girlfriend's identity. It shows inclination and affection. Studying other documents where you need proof of wrongdoing is another example. Also, these handwriting experts will confirm if love letters are from the same person or not. This might be helpful if you need to establish that a long-term, extramarital relationship existed with your spouse. It is not the norm to use handwriting experts, but they can be worth the money if the need arises.

Lie Detection Exams

Do you want to challenge your spouse? Ask them to take a lie detection exam. This works for "Need to Know" clients only. It is not admissible in court. Often, clients don't care about that. They want answers right away. This may be the best route in a small percentage of cases.

An examination that focuses on specifics can get right to the heart of adultery. Question formulation is imperative to address an incident, a specific partner, a night at the local motel and more. Examiners are not always ready to take on non-criminal issues, but I've been successful when tailoring questions to specifics.

No examiner using a lie detector can prove all incidents when your spouse was unfaithful. It's just not possible; it's referred to as "witch hunting." Yet if you know when, where and who participated in adultery, then examiners can perform a test.

Remember, exercising this option will make proving your case in a court of law more difficult. You will have used up all your options right away. If you don't care, then request your spouse take the test. You must have enough information to give to the examiner. A spouse cannot be forced into a test. He must sign a consent form requesting the examination. Otherwise, examiners will not help you. They will not take the chance and risk a lawsuit. If you are not aware of the facts of the affair, this is not an option.

Computer Forensic Services

Computer forensics is a process of establishing the usage of a computer. It is the examination of computer media with the intention to locate, recover, analyze, document and preserve data that is germane to a specific issue. Such records may confirm or refute allegations or suspicious activities. The identification of a correspondent or person(s) involved is a direct benefit of this service.

This new advance enhances your options for evidence collection. Any image, text or file deleted from a hard drive or peripheral drive is retrievable. Files are not completely destroyed or erased but placed aside until written over by other created files. This process may take a year or more to happen.

The assumption by computer users who delete files sent to "recycle bin" is a misnomer. This information is retrievable. The files are actually placed in the unallocated space of the computer's storage area.

Margo's husband Frank was an architect. After work Frank was always using their home computer leaving Margo with all the household duties as well as raising their seven year old daughter. Whenever she approached the home office studio Frank seemed as though he was hiding something. He either turned off the computer monitor or became irritated with her. His behavior signaled to Margo she needed an examination of their computer. She turned to a computer forensic examiner for help.

Shortly after she delivered the computer countless color pictures of naked under aged girls posing provocatively were recovered. Without delay Margo filed for a divorce and sought legal relief for her daughter fearing she was at risk. A family court judge agreed subjecting Frank to one year of psychiatric counseling and restriction from any and all visitation rights. Margo's efforts made a difference in her situation.

When in doubt hiring a computer forensic specialist is well worth the effort.

STEP 4 • WHAT ELSE?

Personal Vehicles

Keeping an eye on your personal vehicles can help determine any activity of adultery. Look for signs of change or evidence inside your cars. You may find hairs, cigarettes in the ashtray, matchbooks, gum wrappers, tissues, lipstick smears, clothing, notes, hairpieces, glasses and more.

Check seating positions. Mark them as a point of reference, especially the passenger seat. Moving this seat forward will reveal where the partner was comfortable in the car. Recline the seat if it moves. Leaving a harmless object on this seat will be another telltale sign.

It's a good idea to check gas consumption. Why? In cold weather, a running motor uses gas while the heater or radio is on.

Mileage

Are you noticing that your cars are consuming more gas than normal? It is possible they are being used for a rendezvous, which would account for the shortage. Start clocking the mileage your spouse drives on a daily basis. Record this information for analysis, and then secure your diary in a place where it will not be found. Verify normal mileage to and from work. Routes may differ for your spouse depending on your part of the country. Be aware of any route changes and traffic conditions throwing off your mileage readings. You may also know that in the morning your spouse drives a pattern that is different from the evening. You will need to know the mileage for each route. Contrast information volunteered by your spouse with what you know to explain any changes. Ask questions when you notice changes.

Keep it simple. For instance: "How was traffic today?" Asking where your spouse ate lunch might prompt details or lead to more facts later. It may take weeks to carefully obtain the information to get a mileage baseline.

Mileage can determine how far your spouse traveled to a particular event or place. It can also disprove an excuse. I often solve a case just by knowing this information. When the numbers don't compute, you are on the right track.

Mileage may furnish you with a pattern of events. It may also tell just how far away the adulterous partner lives or works. Note any patterns that occur on a specific day of the week. You might have a precious piece of information to decipher the riddle. This intelligence will also be useful when you hire an investigator.

Hotel Receipts

We instruct clients who know the hotel in which their spouse stayed to call for a receipt. Clerks will mail copies of the billing for the room, giving away valuable information. The receipt will show if they billed two adults for the room, the method of payment and who paid.

Over the years many hotel bills have shown very incriminating evidence. Are you surprised? After all, any adulterer who uses a hotel or motel has very few explanations for their stay. If your spouse is sleeping at a hotel without you, what possible reason could be plausible?

Handwriting experts compare fictitious names used on hotel registers. They will testify if a possible match with your spouse is found. It's also possible to find the partner's name on the bill. An excuse to the clerks may help in obtaining the receipt. You might first pretend to be the partner. Call back later if that does not work, after the shift change, and instruct the clerk to send the receipt for business records to your post office box.

Surveillance

Clients have conducted their own surveillance work and we can't stop them or make them take our advice. What if you have an accident, or the vehicle breaks down? Are you sure you can be home before your spouse gets there? If you aren't, then the decision to conduct your own field work will work against you.

Another consideration is that you might just discover your spouse is intimate with someone. Can you keep from exploding with rage? In some states, like New York, a spouse is not a competent witness to prove adultery. Don't put yourself in this position - leave it to a professional.

Having prefaced this section with these warnings, some readers will still try to conduct their own surveillance. If you are one of them I have just a few considerations to share. If you plan to conduct surveillance by yourself, renting a car is essential. Borrowing a friend's car or getting them involved is not a good practice. We are not suggesting that you do the surveillance in the first place. On the contrary, bear in mind, you risk legal proof and may compromise an investigation. Sometimes you may be violating stalking laws. When the police officer stops you, what good reason will you have for your actions?

Surveillance of your spouse may end at a hotel, apartment or a private residence. Successful surveillance is typically very difficult for newcomers. One key element is patience. Sitting for hours waiting for activity can be very frustrating. It's easier and better to pay a professional investigator. But if this is not an option, you will need certain items. I realize that when money for a professional is not available, people resort to their own means.

In order to engage in successful surveillance the right equipment is necessary. I have always prepared for surveillance by taking along a cell phone, video recorder, camera(s), binoculars, maps, sufficient gas in the tank, notepad, pens, flashlight, money and coins for tolls, snacks, and reading materials. Disguises such as a pair of glasses and baseball caps can be useful to change your appearance.

The most important time for you to be careful is during the first ten to fifteen minutes of any mobile surveillance. Subjects who are being followed are most aware of their surroundings during that time. This is when they are most likely to look around to see if anyone is watching. After they are on the road for several minutes, it does not matter.

Following too closely is definitely just for television detectives. Don't sit in front of the house under surveillance like they do on television. Unless you are in the city, this never works. If you reside in a rural area, it is very likely that surveillance is difficult unless conducted from a great distance. Finding strategic positions in country settings becomes important.

A surveillance position must be found where the suspect will take the most likely route of departure from your residence, work or meeting place. This decision usually permits surveillance without causing compromise. I've even seen the experts make this common mistake. They get lazy and want to make the job easier by sitting close to a subject's vehicle or house.

Professional investigators use techniques during surveillance to develop evidence. They mark the tires when lovers park cars all night during the affair. I have placed soda cans under tires. This showed me if they backed over them while I was gone for any time. This works when they park facing a house, wall or fence and have to back up. I also put one in front and back of the passenger side tires to cover parking lot situations. Investigators might also purchase a wristwatch with moving hands, place them under tires and note when vehicle movement stopped the watch. This can get expensive for professionals, but you might consider it if the task requires this information.

Constant observation of all exits, such as hotel doors is essential for court testimony. I've placed telltale signs on doors to secure exits. Telltales prove no one entered or left all night unless I witnessed it. Laws in some states require more than one investigator. The second investigator serves as corroboration. Two witnesses establish evidence when testimony is the same. I always use videotape to provide corroboration.

Surveillance is traditionally the means of proving adultery. Just remember: If you blow it, this option may not be available to you anymore. Why risk it? Be careful, because trailing or shadowing your spouse can turn to charges of harassment. This is another reason for you to retain a professional investigator.

Witnesses

Witnesses can be very helpful. They can include friends, employees, and others who have observed your spouse in a compromising situation. You may receive a phone call from a tipster. Make this person a witness if you can. Anyone who has seen your spouse alone with another person of the opposite sex is a candidate.

Witnesses can also include hotel employees, apartment owners or neighbors, security guards on duty at public establishments, bar employees or owners, and so on.

If they were there to see your spouse with another person, they are witnesses. This might include members of the opposite sex who your spouse approached and solicited for sexual intercourse. This can prove inclination. Identification will always come into question. Make sure witnesses can accurately identify your spouse.

If witnesses are neighbors or friends, they may be reluctant to become involved. You may have to compel their attendance by subpoena. This may serve as a cover for them to appear as a hostile witness and get them off the hook with your spouse after the trial. Remember, domestic cases can turn violent. No one wants to get involved out of fear. You can help them and yourself as well, with this option.

You will need to have some idea of what a witness's testimony will be. Going through the time and expense of lawyers, courts and witnesses is not justifiable for insignificant facts. Find out what your witnesses have to offer beforehand. Bringing in witnesses who saw your spouse and his partner together without you can be very valuable.

The Workplace

Since many adulterers have secret relationships at work, you'll need to do some discreet checking. If you have access to your spouse's workplace, make unannounced visits. See how you are received. Do you feel welcome or have open invitations to visit? It's possible you will set off red flags with others there. Who knows, your visit may bring an anonymous phone call to confirm your suspicions.

If you have access to the workplace after hours, go "shopping" and stop in. Check through phone directories; look for notes, appointments and things left behind. Search the desk drawers for love letters. Make this trip very rarely, depending on the operation. It's much easier for those who are self-employed to enter a building after hours. Don't go there if there is an alarm system in the building, because the alarm report will show you were there. This may destroy your entire case.

STEP 5 • TELLTALES

In the investigative trade we use the word "telltale" to describe something that provides us with information. A telltale serves as an indicator of change. In some cases, placing a telltale object in the field of operation will provide needed facts to reach a conclusion.

The purpose of using telltales is to let you in on secret activities. They are inexpensive but very effective. Your choice of telltales is limited only by your imagination and creativity.

A telltale is a visible method of detecting if the door has been opened, the bed was used, if they consumed food or beverages, if clothes were worn, if they walked over rugs, if water was used, or they moved a car.

For instance, leaving a door ajar at a measured distance can show if it was opened. Pushing in chairs up against a table can show if they moved them. Arranging a room or a cabinet tells you about any changes. It's like setting a mousetrap. Eventually you catch the mouse.

A chemical substance catches many a thief when sprayed on stolen currency. A purple dye covers human skin after contact with body oils. Removing this color purple from skin is impossible. Thieves have no excuse.

A perfect example of a telltale is using the chime function on alarm systems. It signals anytime a door or window is opened. The alarm chimes letting you know when someone enters or leaves a house or building. Parents can know when their child comes home from school. Using a telltale will not signal an alarm but tell you if the door was opened. It's the same principle with detection. So, when you need to get proof, simply think of placing a telltale in the way. And letting it work for you.

Let's work this idea a little bit further. If you clean a surface, you will notice changes. New dirt or stains are easily found. Put objects in the way to show you if someone moves them. It's like counting the number of cookies in the bag to see if the kids took them. You might place a mark on a beverage container to find out if someone drank from it. Bar owners used to do this to check on employees before automation and new technology was developed to detect inventory shrinkage.

This principle of detection works in many situations. If you have access and opportunity to use telltales, make it a regular habit. Just be careful.

Now let's consider where to use telltales. Any time you leave the house, place several telltales where they will tell you something. Using your creativity, you can detect if the back door was opened. Pull out a hair from your head and tape it to both the door and the jam. Use clear tape. Put it on the lower section to avoid detection. If the door was opened, one end of the hair will no longer be attached.

Move things around so that they are in the way but not obviously. Placing a pillow on the couch in a certain way will show someone moved it.

Telltales give you a tool. The cleverer you are with them, the better the results of your investigation.

CHAPTER SIX

PRIVATE INVESTIGATORS

"ADVICE IS SELDOM WELCOME, AND THOSE WHO
NEED IT THE MOST, LIKE IT THE LEAST."
LORD CHESTERFIELD

" **F**or you, my daughter, I will arrange the finest wedding ever," boasted Terry's father. When he made promises like that, he meant it. His computer business was extremely lucrative so he had the means to pull off just such an event.

Mr. Dunn set out to show all his family, friends and colleagues, what a real wedding should look like. He rented a castle, a full orchestra, the finest food court, and everyone rode in a limo. Everyone!

Terry spent hours a day on the phone telling friends and acquaintances about the big day. She bragged to those she knew could be counted on to spread news and gossip, and even boasted of her good fortune to the ones she knew would be most envious. It was not nice, but Terry always played that game well.

In early May the church bells rang out the joyous sounds of her wedding. Phil had loved Terry since high school. After graduating from college for engineering, he returned home. Terry was still available and very much interested in him. They had a long engagement. Phil wanted to be sure of this commitment. Terry's family fell head over heels for him. He was athletic, good looking and on his way to a successful career. His family also had money, so he was a perfect match for their only girl.

Terry lived a privileged life. She enjoyed her time with Phil and his humor. He was always the entertainer and life of the party. Terry kept him at bay when she needed time for herself. To Phil this was just Terry, a little terse but harmless. He loved the outdoors, hunting and fishing. Taking trips with his family was a way of life. They vacationed in national parks, renting cabins, camping under the stars and living without boundaries. Terry seldom found his outdoor expeditions necessary. Camping meant a luxury hotel near the park with room service and a pool. She joked when he suggested they would "see the sights." Phil was talented and resourceful. He was never stumped by obstacles, they were just challenges. Terry preferred to let someone else "deal with it." Soon they were to marry and enjoy a life together.

Before they knew it the day arrived. The weather that day was excellent; with sunshine all morning and no chance of rain. Mr. Dunn felt like a king and his wife, Elizabeth, could have taken the queen's place easily. She radiated charm and privilege. They left the estate ready to make this day the best. By day's end they would feel so proud of their daughter and themselves for spending $500,000.00. Not too many executives would spend this much, but this was Dunn's way of proving he had made it.

It seemed nothing was left out, or would go wrong. The rehearsal dinner was still on everyone's minds, so the wedding seemed a sure winner.

Phil and Terry's wedding ceremony at the church was nothing short of riveting. Mr. Dunn and his wife loved every moment. It was a glorious event. He gave away his precious daughter and had to hold back the tears. She could do nothing wrong in his eyes.

Leaving the church, limo after limo streamed to the park for photographs of the wedding party. The photographers captured this festive event and spectacular location. It was every photographer's dream - especially the budget that they were given. No one wanted to leave but the reception hall was ready. The castle gave this day such a feel of romance. A full array of armed guards in knights' garments was impressive. Dunn made sure the photographers captured this touch. He had thought of it himself.

Inside the grand ballroom, music set the atmosphere and the smell of fine food could not be finer. A ring of the bell by the master of ceremonies announced Phil and Terry as "husband and wife." The guests applauded and cheered. Some of the women cried at this marvelous event. The tables were all dressed with fine china, 24K gold utensils and a stunning bouquet of flowers.

Everyone was seated when Carl, the best man, offered a toast to Phil and Terry. Carl had known both of them since high school. His words flattered them and brought Terry to tears. When she started to cry, so did most of the women. They were moved by her emotions.

Carl sat down and felt pretty proud of his choice of words. He always had a way of touching people with his charm. Carl dazzled many women in his day, but never found the right woman.

Phil seemed very touched by Carl's toast. Standing up, every eye was on him. This day was remarkable and it seemed as though it would never end. He said "Mom, Dad, Mr. & Mrs. Dunn, honored guests; I have a surprise for each one of you. If you will turn over your plates you will find a photograph. Tomorrow I am having this marriage annulled." With that shocking statement he walked out of the dining hall.

Horror filled the reception hall as plate after plate was lifted up. His bride, Terry, and Carl, his best man, were captured on film in bed together the week before the wedding. Phil had hired a private investigator when he suspected something was wrong with his relationship. Instead of calling off the wedding, Phil wanted the whole world to know the truth about Terry and Carl.

ᔓᎧᏒ

DO I REALLY NEED AN INVESTIGATOR?

Clients hire private investigators for two main reasons; first, you want to satisfy a NEED TO KNOW. You need to confirm suspicions. Most of my clients fit into this category. They want to make sound decisions based on facts. Investigations focused just on satisfying your "need to know" are often less expensive as they require less evidence. You will spend less money if you just need to confirm your suspicions and determine the identity of adulterous partners.

Secondly, victims want to obtain competent LEGAL EVIDENCE and pursue the matter in a court of law. Very often adultery proven in child custody cases brings a heavy price tag for those caught. Women lose their custody rights. Fathers gain support payments.

Many custody and marital cases have benefited from the aid of an investigator. They serve as professional witnesses in the court's eyes. You cannot have a family member conduct investigations. They are considered biased.

Again, we prove evidence of adultery when we meet certain legal criteria. This means showing inclination, intent and opportunity. Elaborate words, but they mean that evidence of adultery documents an outward sign of affection, a rendezvous, and a time and place for sexual activity to occur. Usually the partners are alone in a house, apartment, motel, hotel or vehicle long enough-without lighting or others present-to have a sexual encounter. It usually occurs at night.

Some states are more lenient than others. Most states only require "circumstantial evidence." It is no longer necessary to contrive a raid, obtain a warrant and observe the parties involved in the sexual acts. Yet today, with electronic recording gear, you can now capture this telling evidence if it is within your own home. You have legal rights to you own premises.

Hiring an investigator is a good idea. The next step is finding one and making the right choice. So let's focus on hiring an investigator.

In any business, ethics plays a role in what services we receive. The investigative business has its share of charlatans.

FINDING A REPUTABLE INVESTIGATOR

Most private investigators are easy to find in the yellow pages under "Detectives, Security or Investigators." Many investigators have no experience in domestic relations cases. Not every investigative office is prepared, equipped or knowledgeable in the art of catching lovers. If you are not selective, bad investigators can make the situation worse. Just as with any occupation, finding a good investigator requires proper research.

This step will require some homework. Selecting an investigator or a private investigative agency can be risky. Dishonest investigators take retainers and do nothing in return. They waste funds and accomplish nothing. This may result from either inexperience or lack of integrity. Remember you are paying for a service, just like an attorney, accountant, computer repair service or car mechanic. Reputation is vital to your choice. How many of us have used local contractors and wasted money? The reputable investigators always have work. It makes sense that they should.

Start by searching the names of investigators you are interested in hiring at your local county Clerks' civil action records. When someone brings a civil action against an investigator or his business, a record is made. You can research these civil actions yourself. Records of lawsuits, liens and judgments are available in every county. The logical county to search is where the investigator has an office address. Some investigators work from their homes. Still, you can research records within that county seat to be safe. If you have difficulty researching, ask the clerk to help you search for the name, both business and personal. This will tell you of any past civil actions in which they were involved. If you find a file, read through the court case, take note of what it says and see if this helps your decision.

As you shop around, ask investigators how long your state agency has licensed them. Ask them if they ever testified in a domestic case. Ask them for the names of attorneys they work for in this field. Obtain names of attorneys representing parties in cases they worked for or gave testimony. Even if you do nothing more than request the information, you will find out if they have any experience in the field. Ask them the names of local family court judges. Verify judges' names they give you. Also, ask when they gave testimony and what evidence was presented. Let me share an experience with you to explain what can happen if you are not careful.

❧❦

There is a moral to this story. A very young and attractive female client made an appointment with me to find her maternal father. On her own, she was having trouble making any progress. We met just once. I did not hear from her again until several weeks later. She decided to use a lower-priced investigator she discovered through shopping the yellow pages. He agreed to work for her at less than half my price. She made an appointment with him. He took a retainer, and then ran a basic computer search that produced no useful information for Karen.

Since he operated from his house, he would meet her at restaurants or parking lots. Naturally he obtained her home address, date of birth, phone number and marital status. She was single. I was familiar with his low-ball tactics from clients who had dealt with him previously. Coupled with the money factor, my client reported receiving late night calls from him where he sounded intoxicated. This turned her off right away.

In Karen's case he seemed interested in her plight at first. He came to her apartment to review the computer search report but seemed to stay too long. She was uncomfortable with him being in her apartment so she ended their meeting and showed him the door. The next day she answered the phone and he wanted to come back. His reasoning appeared shallow and she gave him an excuse. He called one more time that week and said he had some information to give her. This time Karen made certain she was not alone. Her girlfriend stayed that night and witnessed the next encounter.

He showed up with a piece of paper that made no sense and told Karen how her submissive astrological sign was compatible to his very aggressive sign. He told her they were destined for each other. Karen kicked him out and closed the chapter on his services. She let the phone ring that night. Finally, Karen moved out of state after finding another job that would put distance between them.

$\mathcal{T}$HE MORE YOU KNOW

Unfortunately for Karen, she ran out of money and could not retain us. The moral is "cheaper is not always better." In my experience doing a bit of background research is prudent.

To help you in this search we have assembled details for contacting state agencies from all fifty states. In *"State Agencies Licensing Private Investigators"* in the back of the book, we've compiled a comprehensive list of websites, addresses (street/mailing), contact phones and fax lines. Use this list to verify, locate or select an investigator in your area. Some state websites provide a complete list of licensed investigators by name or city. This information will be useful in your selection of a reputable investigator.

HERE ARE SOME GUIDELINES

Consider the following guidelines to improve your chances of success. By using them you eliminate the possibility that you will be charged for this information.

First, if you know a reputable domestic relations lawyer, call and ask for a referral. Just because an investigator was a former police officer doesn't mean he can conduct domestic relations investigations. It is one of the hardest types of investigations to do correctly.

Second, if you know of a reputable investigator who works in your area, make an appointment. Possibly a friend has hired one before and was very pleased with the services. Any professional investigator who has a reputation of working odd hours, late nights and with little notice is worth considering. They are more likely to be honest and ethical.

At the beginning, find out about conflicts of interest. They are ethically supposed to tell you if they cannot take the assignment due to a conflict. They may work for your spouse's attorney in some way or know your spouse well enough to affect their services to you.

The investigator's job is to listen to you. He must get a great deal of facts from you to get results. Also, you don't want to pay them to get information you already know.

Investigators must have good video and photographic equipment. They must not engage in illegal activities or invade someone's privacy. Their contract should spell this out clearly. Any violation of local, state or federal laws can only hurt your case. Investigators with integrity already have a clause stating that they do not violate laws to obtain information. When it is missing, beware; this is a glaring warning omission.

THE FEES AND CONTRACT

When it comes to fees, ask for a copy of their contract up front. See if they explain the financial terms. Does their contract leave an open-ended billing arrangement? They should give you an estimated budget in writing, limiting your financial obligation to their services. In New York, the law requires that private investigators place all their fees and budgets in writing. However, this is not so everywhere.

You may want to have an attorney look over their contract before signing it. If the investigator has any problem with your asking, politely excuse yourself and run. Don't be afraid to ask about their fees.

A good investigator is professional in demeanor and a good

communicator, both verbally and in writing. They are going to testify for you, so you want someone who makes a good appearance. They need to contribute to your success. It makes sense for you to be selective.

Fees vary according to demand for their services and locality. We normally require a retainer up front to support the investigation. A written contract will keep you from a surprise bill at the end.

All pertinent information must be part of the investigator's contract. This includes fees, services, reporting and compliance issues. Some states require a contract to include the name of the licensing department for the protection of consumers. Yellow page ads post the name and telephone numbers for those agencies. Don't hesitate to call them and verify the license status of the investigator you want to hire. There are internet sites available to search in your state posting this information. Again, it is prudent for you to complete a bit of research before hiring professional help, not just an investigator.

Again, a little research is prudent for you to complete before contracting anyone, not just investigators. After all you are obligated to the terms of the resulting contract. When it comes to fees, you may need to borrow money from a bank, family member or credit card to hire the investigator.

Use the checklist in the back when you are considering hiring a private investigator.

CHAPTER SEVEN

TEN STEPS TO REBUILD YOUR FUTURE

"BE SLOW OF TONGUE AND QUICK OF EYE."
MIGUEL DE CERVANTES

"AMONG MORTALS SECOND THOUGHTS ARE WISEST."
EURIPIDES

The most important phase in managing information about adultery is how you react. Let's say you have ironclad proof your spouse has committed adultery. What will you do at this point? Consider the following strategies:

STEP 1 — STAY CALM

You must stay calm and in control of your feelings. It is essential. Dodge situations that stir up your emotions and cause you to jeopardize what you know.

This heartache will pass with time. Optimistically, you will be done with this crisis in a year or so. You will have fewer issues to deal with as you control your emotions. Thinking with your head will keep you out of more predicaments. You might find someone to confide in right away who can help you, not make matters worse. Seek support from a levelheaded, objective person.

STEP 2!
LEAVE CHILDREN OUT OF IT!

Children are being hurt already by adultery. Using them for information to help your cause is wrong. Involving them in your problems robs them of their self-esteem and freedom. They will appreciate what you did for them when they are old enough to understand. You do not have to prove your victimization to them. They will find that out in time.

Expect monumental problems if you bring your children into your divorce proceedings. You will face continuous issues and many too big to solve if you cross the line. It is not worth it. Be conscientious of how much they see, hear and know about your dilemma.

STEP 3
DON'T RETALIATE!

Retaliation is out of the question. Your character is also under investigation in court. One mistake and you are finished. Retaliation does not heal. It only makes matters worse. It clouds issues and creates more problems. Don't add to your situation. If you hope to reconcile there is no room for nasty rumors, true or not, or engaging in a "payback" affair. Think twice before you act. Control your feelings.

STEP 4 — SHARE YOUR EXPERIENCE

Consider seeking help from a clinical psychologist, marriage counselor, clergyman or other professional. A very close friend may help you, but be careful. Again, I do not recommend confiding in family. You will always have issues to deal with if you do. You will need to talk with someone who really cares. Make it clear how important your privacy is to you, your children and your future.

Divorce is not always the answer when infidelity is discovered. Looking at the grander picture will help you decide what to do next. Most importantly, do not share your evidence if you plan to file for divorce. When someone appears to make a new start of it, promising to be faithful, the best word of advice I can give is "caution." Assessing your spouse's personality, motives, family history, and present circumstances are very important. If the sudden act of repentance is by word only without action it's worthless. Yet, if your spouse remains repentant for weeks, be open to reconciliation. Consider the actions for they indicate the condition of one's heart. "For out of the heart, the mouth speaks" says the Bible.

STEP 5 — KNOW WHAT YOU WANT

After you have gathered evidence of adultery, decide what you want from your relationship. Some have stuck it out and others just needed to confirm their suspicions and move on. It is a personal and spiritual choice for you to make.

Courtroom battles are not without personal sacrifices. You always stand the chance of losing. Still, with proof, your chances of winning are better. Only you can decide when and if to use the facts.

Some clients choose not to use the evidence I have uncovered. They change their minds. Maybe their spouse came clean. Hope may surface again after a confession. Consider the counsel from people you respect and trust. Be cautious and do what you know is best.

I've always suggested to clients that they list conditions for the adulterer to live up to. These are ground rules and terms that they must strictly obey. This will tell you if you have any hope of continuing with the marriage. If they do not readily agree to these terms, don't expect the leopard to change its spots!

Having ground rules is important. For instance, knowing daily schedules or plans, limit travel alone, plus diligent communications each day may be reasonable. Placing a ball and chain around your spouse is not possible and is not a marriage. Yet making some good-faith rules will help you build trust again.

It is safe to say that lovers who admit they violated the marriage bed before getting caught have a better chance of being a trusted mate in the future. On the other hand, those we catch before the confession will most likely do it again.

In some states the first one caught in adultery has no legal recourse. They cannot catch their spouse in adultery as a counterclaim. Also, the forgiveness clause may be invoked when a spouse receives back the adulterer by having physical intimacy after obtaining knowledge of the event.

In a court of law, negotiations are critical. Keeping this evidence secret until just the right time wins more custody cases or settles them faster. Use evidence wisely, fairly and with good intentions. In cases where adultery plays into custody matters, evidence of adultery will prove useful.

STEP 6
WATCH THE REBOUNDS

In the sport of basketball, like so many other sports, athletes score by concentrating on rebounds. A rebound is anticipating a deflection of the ball that does not go through the net for a score. It may strike the rim or backboard and fall to the floor below. A competitor will look for this mistake and retrieve the ball, shoot again and hopefully score. Often, teams win games by the number of rebounds they achieve. Statisticians incorporate rebounds as a category for measuring a team and player's performance. Rebounding is a positive accomplishment and a great offensive strategy. This is true in other sports like soccer, lacrosse and field hockey to mention just a few. Why bring this subject up?

The urge to fill a void in one's heart and life can be very compelling. Unfortunately, some people seek to fill this need far too quickly, starting a new relationship soon after ending another. However, rebounding from one relationship to the next is a poor choice and almost always a failed strategy. At the close of a relationship it's a natural inclination to move hastily and seek another. I believe it's done without much thought but purely by emotion. More often than not you will experience an unsuccessful relationship. Allowing time for healing is very positive and essential to an emotionally healthy future. Take a life pause and wait to begin another commitment. It's not only sensible, it is wise. Proceed with caution and ask yourself some questions. "Am I going too fast with this relationship? Is this new relationship an attempt to find closure or eradicate the anguish caused by my spouse's infidelity?" If your answer is yes, a new relationship at once is not the answer. Remember, your priority is healing. Take the time necessary to heal. Only you can discern how much time is needed. You may decide not to seek another relationship for quite some time. That choice clearly is prudent for many. The right choice in any case is up to you.

STEP 7 — YOU'VE GOT MAIL

Check with your local post office for the availability of a box rental. It comes in handy when you need documents sent to you without being detected at home. You can safely receive legal papers, bills or other reports at your post office box. Your spouse cannot get into that box without your permission.

Also, some detective agencies can learn if your spouse has opened a box to hide mail or important documents from you. Maybe a trip to the post office in the morning will show your spouse is making a visit for mail.

I have seen an adulterer take all the marital assets by hiding bank accounts and other funds during their affairs. He anticipated a departure and set up a new address. The adulterer will get a post office box without their trusting spouse's knowledge. So, look for any mail with a return address from a post office box.

STEP 8
THE ELEMENT OF SURPRISE

Using the element of surprise is very beneficial. The evidence, either obtained by you or a professional investigator, is best used with some surprise timing. Why? Let's say your spouse has a reckless attitude and is not thinking rationally. As your legal situation unfolds, it may put you in a better position just by waiting them out. Revealing all that you know too soon will not have the desired impact on your spouse or legal representative. Don't give away any information to family or friends who might compromise your case.

You may want to hide the fact that you've hired a private investigator until the last possible moment. For example, acting in unison with a client's attorney, my name has been kept off the witness list until the day of trial. Sometimes I was a surprise witness. This turned heads. It worked to my client's advantage. Clients possessing solid evidence of adultery must keep it secret until court hearings. It leverages the other side to act or deal with you. If they don't, you continue with the court case and win. I've been labeled an "insurance policy" by attorneys.

The timing for using evidence is important. Very often playing your hand with the element of surprise is very beneficial. Being protective and secretive about your evidence is vital. Save it for the right time and watch what it does.

STEP 9
COMPOSE TWO RESPONSES

What do you say to people when they ask about your troubled relationship? Is it prudent to tell everyone about the crisis you are experiencing? Since your whole world is now turned upside down, not to mention the fact that many friendships with family and friends could quickly come to an end, you might be tempted to verbally blast your spouse's deeds to the world.

Here's what you can do instead. Visualize walking through your neighborhood, releasing the contents of a feather pillow during a blustery fall day. Certainly feathers will scatter endlessly across lawns, in trees, and atop roofs, resting wherever they land. Now imagine you had to recover every one of those feathers or face criminal charges. This would certainly be a monumental task. Of course, the same difficult task arises when we circulate -(they're not rumors, they're true) negative stories about people. We can't take back those words once they're out. We can't fix the hurt we spread. If we're not careful, no matter how eloquent our vocabulary, our words can hurt someone.

With that in mind, recognize that you will struggle with moments when an explanation—though not every sordid detail—is very important to you or your situation. To alleviate any potential problems caused by saying too much or the wrong thing, and to better manage your personal affairs, try answering any questions with a question, like "Why do you ask?" This way you retain control of the conversation, keep your replies positive, and shift the attention focused on generalities rather than specifics you choose to reveal.

Also, take time to create answers for different situations or people—one for your closest family members and friends, another for your public life, etc. Your inner circle of close friends, family, and relatives want specifics; they are entitled to know how you are doing. They want answers to satisfy their "need to know" just as you were compelled during your discovery phase. How much information you share is a matter of who is asking. Think damage control. If you offer too much information, there's always a risk of losing confidentiality. In addition, you may be misunderstood or, worse, your facts may turn out to be mistakenly or intentionally distorted. In either case new problems surface, so avoid this pitfall.

If there are children involved in your marriage, keep in mind they will face inevitable hardships as the result of a divorce. It is prudent to take the "high road," and model the highest character. When you possess an optimistic outlook, so will your children. If you demonstrate a hopeful attitude, they will be more likely to do the same. This is very healthy behavior for them to see and copy, as they may one day face a similar crisis in their lives. Your example will be the foundation for their resilience, character, and positive choices.

You can be ready for any situation and any question by simply being prepared. You can even jot down several prepared responses to the questions you are most asked or most anticipate. For example, you can explain how you had hoped your marriage or relationship would work out better.

As a final point, consider preparing a message for your public, fellow employees, and social circle. In the days ahead you will encounter those who worry about you, others who will seek out any rumors, or those who are merely bound to seek an explanation when they learn your marriage has ended. You will diffuse any discomfort to you or the possibility of rumors with a simple, kind, and polite answer. Also, by doing so, you will keep inquirers at a distance without compromising your reputation. Again, take the time to write down how you might answer them. It's worth your time.

STEP 10
REBUILD OR MOVE ON?

Infidelity can destroy a relationship. For some individuals, it ends the marriage. Survivors will face great challenges trying to make the marriage last. It will come with a high price tag. You must have a forgiving heart to stay married.

The right choice depends on the circumstances and the adulterer. Seeking professional help is most important.

CHAPTER EIGHT
A FINAL WORD

"TO ERR IS HUMAN, TO FORGIVE, DIVINE."
ALEXANDER POPE

In Samuel G. Kling's book, The Complete Guide to Everyday Law, Third Edition, (c) 1973, Follett Publishing Company, Chicago, Illinois, page 60 it reads:

> "What is to be said for remaining unhappily married? You at least know what you have, which is possibly more than you may expect in the next marriage. An unhappy marriage may also offer compensatory advantages in terms of status, prestige, finances, and acceptance by the community. It is often the line of least resistance, since it requires little energy or exertion . . . Some people are gluttons for punishment; they would be miserable, paradoxically, if they were not unhappy."

His words may work for you, or they may be too harsh. Each marriage and situation is different. We are all different and unique. One thing is clear - you need to heal. To do this, you need others. You must go on.

From the start I've pointed out many important insights I've gleaned while satisfying clients' curiosity. Understanding what types of relationships are vulnerable illuminates the need for caution. Knowing when a behavior is a warning sign allows the observer to respond accordingly. Opportunities to capture or prove infidelity come and go. The techniques and information I have shared will narrow your search for the truth.

Both victims and perpetrators dictate the future by their choices. The victim may choose to forgive but not forget or take appropriate legal measures or demand whatever is necessary to heal and rebuild the relationship. Taking time to reestablish and enjoy the company of your mate is a must. Avoid locations that remind you or your mate of the past; instead, make new memories.

The unfaithful partner severs the truth. Mending a ripped tapestry is very difficult if not almost impossible to do, but it can be done. Needless to say the work requires commitment. Honesty is vital and may be painful; there are no shortcuts for the unfaithful. What brought you to the place of infidelity is worth seeking. Your spouse needs to see repentance from you. How is that done? You must paint a new canvas each day reflecting love, commitment and reassurance. Otherwise, hope fades and the end is inevitable for your marriage.

Being victimized creates the need for healing. Hope can still arise in your situation no matter how bad things get. Try to find good in your life and world. Time will help you heal from being victimized. Most crimes involve a perpetrator and a victim. Adultery is a crime against marriage and society. Unfortunately, courts do not handle it that way anymore. In some states, it is still a felony. Sad to say, no one wants to press the issue.

Surviving adultery is very difficult. You will face many tiring battles. When you do, expect a gauntlet of emotions, especially while trying to expose adultery. Part of this experience will be emotional pain that others may never understand. Therefore, you must seek help. You deserve to heal!

My wife Linda has coined this phrase. I hope it encourages you. We repeat it continually when facing challenges: "It's not what you are going through, but how you go through it." I genuinely hope this book will help your circumstances.

Finally, try prayer . . . You're never really alone!

VITAL STATISTICS

Documenting statistics of deaths, marriages, divorces and births is an on-going process for federal and state agencies. These events are easily monitored, evaluated and analyzed later on. To the contrary accurate records on infidelity are not being tracked and can not be accomplished, especially with so many states going to "no-fault" divorces. Accurately obtaining data for research of adulterous activities, its' causes, background and scope, is impossible.

For the past three decades I have witnessed first hand and documented activities of cheating spouses. I've tracked their movements, behaviors, techniques, deception and mistakes. As a result of my extensive investigative work in this field I have compiled these statistics:

ABOUT MARRIAGES AND DIVORCE:

• 50-60 percent of all American marriages end in divorce.

• Within the last decade, incidents of adultery have risen at the alarming rate of as much as 50-70 percent in America.

• 100 percent of extramarital affairs take their toll on biological and stepchildren

ABOUT THE ADULTERERS:

• 100 percent of the time adulterers violate the trust they shared and enjoyed with their spouse.

- 99.99 percent of adulterers deny they are having an affair and hide the truth!

- 80-85 percent who initiate a confession to their spouse recover and enjoy a stronger marriage afterwards.

- 10-20 percent of cheating begins as an internet affair in chatrooms or at game websites.

- 75 percent of adulterers are middle-class wage earners.

- 60-70 percent of adultery victims are women.

- 10-15 percent of female victims are between the ages of 20-25 years old.

- 50-75 percent of female victims are between the ages of 25-50 years old.

- 3-5 percent of female victims are married more than 25 years to the same spouse.

- 30-40 percent of adultery victims are men. This number has increased dramatically over the past decade and a half, due in part to the increased presence of women in the workplace.

- 15-20 percent of cheaters are repeat offenders.

ADULTERY AND THE CHURCH:

- 20-25 percent of adultery victims claim to be Christians, and the cheating spouse usually is a regular attendant of church or religious activities.

- 3-5 percent of adulterers are pastors or clergy.

- 90-95 percent of affairs involving clergy divide churches causing spiritual upheaval within their sphere of influence. Many congregants become skeptical, bitter and resentful when their public trust is violated.

ABOUT THE AFFAIR:

- 50-75 percent of extramarital affairs take place with an individual in or around the workplace.

- 70-80 percent of the time, extramarital activity lasts six months to a year but not longer.

- 50 percent of extramarital affairs take place under cover of darkness or in the shadow of night.

- 40-50 percent of adulterers frequent motels or hotels.

- 40-50 percent of sexual activity occurs in a residence, apartment, or office location.

- 30-50 percent of affairs involve alcohol during their indiscretions.

- 50-75 percent of extramarital affairs occur on weekends.

- 10-15 percent of marriages survive affairs after professional or non-professional (clergy) counseling where the act of forgiveness occurs.

- 25-40 percent of spouses having affairs bring financial ruin to their marital home.

- 10-15 percent of affairs result in physical abuse with their spouse at some stage of the affair.

- 80-90 percent of domestic relations investigations reveal evidence of adultery when one spouse questions the other's devotion and loyalty.

- 80-90 percent of marriages consummated as a result of an

affair fail.

QUESTIONNAIRE

Take this quick test to determine if you may be a victim of adultery. Check each box that applies to your situation and compare your total score with the score sheet.

- ❑ Are you having a tough time communicating with your spouse?
- ❑ Does your spouse disappear without a good excuse?
- ❑ Does your marriage seem to be slipping away?
- ❑ Have you been suspicious of your spouse's sexual habits?
- ❑ Is the intimacy less than normal?
- ❑ Does your spouse argue when you ask for an explanation of his/her whereabouts?
- ❑ Are the simple things, like getting bills paid on time or spending time together, not important to your spouse anymore?
- ❑ Is there a problem with money?
- ❑ Do you notice more unexplained ATM transactions?
- ❑ Are you not invited on business trips?
- ❑ Have you noticed more mileage on your spouse's vehicle that does not add up?
- ❑ Has your spouse begun to have an interest in hobbies that don't involve you?
- ❑ Are you feeling a real distance in your relationship?
- ❑ Have you received numerous hang-up phone calls?

- ❑ Does your spouse get touchy when you ask to use his private cell phone?

- ❑ Are there unexplained phone numbers on the cell phone?

- ❑ Does your spouse want to be alone more often?

- ❑ Do you find it difficult to get your spouse to attend social events with you?

- ❑ Have you been embarrassed by your spouse when he displays affection to someone else in public?

- ❑ Have you received an anonymous call or letter about your spouse's extramarital activities?

- ❑ Do you feel like denying things are wrong with your marriage?

- ❑ Have you noticed any major changes in your spouse's appearance?

- ❑ Has your spouse changed his/her personality?

- ❑ Are you feeling insecure?

- ❑ Can you describe your marriage as a struggle?

- ❑ Are you feeling inadequate as a spouse?

- ❑ Do you get excuses too often when your spouse comes home late?

- ❑ Do you fight constantly?

- ❑ Does your spouse put you down all the time?

- ❑ Have you found love letters or notes to your spouse?

- ❑ Is your spouse preoccupied with sex?

- ❑ Does your spouse make regular excuses and refrain from sexual activity with you?

- ❑ You often notice atypical erratic behavior by your spouse.

❏ The wedding ring is not worn.

❏ A "glow" comes over her.

❏ Mutual friends become distant or act strangely toward you.

❏ He stops confiding in you or seeking advice.

❏ He shows a sudden interest in new styles of music.

❏ You find she buys a cell phone and didn't let you know.

❏ He sets up a separate cell phone account billed to the office.

❏ She buys a pre-paid cell phone without your knowledge

❏ He claims not to know whose cell phone it is that you found in his vehicle or briefcase.

❏ Does your spouse make regular excuses and refrain from sexual activity with you?

❏ The amount of money being deposited into your checking account shrinks without a plausible explanation.

❏ He becomes "accusatory," asking if you are being true to him, usually out of guilt.

❏ Do you get excuses too often when your spouse comes home late?

❏ He insists the child seat, toys, etc., have no place in his car.

❏ He abruptly participates with the laundry.

❏ New love techniques are tried.

❏ He/she fairly suddenly stops having sex with you, without good reason.

❏ He/she suddenly wants more sex, more often.

❏ Picks fights in order to stomp out of the house.

❏ You discover by accident he or she took vacation day or personal time off from work - but supposedly worked on those days.

❑ The pay stub never reflects all the overtime.

❑ Spouse's co-workers are uncomfortable in your presence.

❑ He spends an excessive amount of time on the computer, especially after you have gone to bed.

❑ She deletes all incoming e-mails when they used to accumulate.

❑ Certain incoming caller information is deleted from the caller ID box.

❑ She always has her cell phone turned off after leaving the home and the excuses don't add up.

❑ A new e-mail account is opened and but you are not told about it.

❑ He or she has a sudden preoccupation with appearance.

❑ You find intimate apparel or other small gift-type items you did not give your spouse.

❑ Your spouse seems less comfortable around you and is "touchy" and easily moved to anger.

❑ You receive calls where the caller hangs up when your voice is heard.

❑ A low voice or whisper is used on the phone or she hangs up quickly as you enter the room.

❑ She has a loss of attention to the activities in the home.

❑ A definite change in attitude toward everyone in the home becomes obvious.

❑ She sleeps with her purse by the bed.

❑ He tells you to reach him at a different telephone number.

❑ Did you or your spouse experience the effects of adultery

during your childhood?

❏ Your intuition—gut feeling—tells you something is amiss with your relationship.

SCORING

❑ 0-3   Your marriage is in good health.

❑ 4-5   A slim possibility of adultery exists.

❑ 6-7   You may be a victim.

❑ 8-10   It's likely you are a victim.

❑ 11-15   Most likely you are a victim.

❑ 16-25   High likelihood you are a victim.

❑ 25 +   Seek professional help.

PRIVATE INVESTIGATOR CHECKLIST

Before you meet with the investigator,
consider this checklist:

❏ Get a recent picture of your spouse, one that your spouse will not miss.

❏ Identify your spouse's vital statistics, like date of birth, Social Security number, a maiden name and previous marriages.

❏ Provide a physical description including; height, weight, eye and hair color, glasses, facial hair, hair style and length, and any mannerisms.

❏ Record the type of vehicle(s) your spouse drives, including the registration number. You might take a picture of it to give the investigator.

❏ Assemble a list of places your spouse is known to frequent, including homes of relatives and friends, work locations, bars, and clubs. If the investigator loses your spouse during surveillance, he can quickly start searching these places. On many late nights, I pinpointed where an adulterer was and did not have to end the investigation, because I had this information.

❏ Give telephone numbers for your spouse and a way to contact you when needed. You might invest in phone cards during the investigation because they leave no trace of your call to the investigator.

❏ Give them the name and background of the adulterous partner, if known. It saves you when the investigator knows whom to look for; he won't have to waste time finding out what you already know. Nevertheless, remember, don't play detective. You may pay more in the end or blow the case.

❏ Give a schedule when you want the investigator to work.

Make certain your investigator is available on days you need him. Last minute planning may not be possible, but a good investigator will try to fit your needs.

❑ The purpose of hiring an investigator is to obtain video or photographic evidence. Also, they can get copies of motel receipts or other similar documentation to testify for you. Investigators will try to document any sign of activity between your spouse and the partner. Testimony by an investigator is also damaging to the adulterer. He must record any observation of the adulterous couple together without you.

❑ Get fees in writing before you retain an investigator. Expect to pay an hourly fee, mileage, out-of-pocket (direct expenses) like tolls, copies of court records, and video or photographic charges. This is normal in the business. Your job is to have all the homework done before engaging their services. In this way you save considerable funds.

❑ Hire the investigator for specific dates to control the costs. You may even go out of town on purpose, setting the stage for your spouse to be alone. You are not condoning or contributing to adultery. The acts of your spouse, when committing adultery, will go on despite your actions.

❑ Be careful when using the phone. Your spouse may have connected a tape recorder to review your calls, keeping an eye on you. This gives the adulterer the edge on what you know. Also, when you call your investigator from home, dial another number immediately afterwards so your spouse does not redial your investigator's number. All your plans could come apart with this simple mistake. If it is a toll call, do not use your phone without a phone card.

❑ Do not tell family members about your suspicions or actions. Trusting them may lead to bigger issues. It has opened hurts that rarely heal.

STATE AGENCIES LICENSING PRIVATE INVESTIGATORS

This list represents state licensing agencies throughout the United States and is provided for informational purposes only. Listed below are state websites, agency contact information and experience required to obtain a private investigators license. When no state agency exists, the state Private Investigative Association was substituted. You may use this contact information to verify an investigator's name, license, address or status prior to contacting one.

NOTE: We make reference to acronyms after each state name which indicates the type of license required to operate as a private investigator in those states. They are **OLR** (*Occupational License Required*); **BLR** (*Business License Required*); **SLR** (*State License Required*) or **NLR** (*No License Required*).

ALABAMA—(OLR)—http://www.alabama.gov/
License Commission, Courthouse 109 Government, Mobile, AL 36602
http://www.ador.state.al.us/licenses/sec093.html
Experience: None. To become a PI in Alabama, pay the license fee.

ALASKA—(BLR)—http://www.state.ak.us/
State of Alaska, Department of Law, State Capitol, Juneau, AK 99811
No statues or regulations govern private investigators in Alaska.
Private investigators are subject to the same general laws as are all citizens.
Experience: None

ARKANSAS—(BLR)—http://www.state.ar.us/
Arkansas State Police—Board of Private Investigators & Private Security Agencies, NO 3 Natural Resources Drive, P.O. Box 5901, Little Rock, AR 72215
http://www.state.ar.us/directory/detail2.cgi?ID=1083
Experience: For both investigative and security applicants: two years related experience.

ARIZONA—(SLR)—http://www.az.gov/webapp/portal/
Arizona Department of Public Safety, Phoenix, AR 85005   Phone: (602) 223-2361
http://www.dps.state.az.us/cjsd/licensingbureau/licensingbureau.htm
Experience: For both investigative and security applicants: two years related experience.

CALIFORNIA—(SLR)—http://www.state.ca.us/
Department of Consumer, Affairs Licensing Division, P.O. Box 98900,
West Sacramento, CA 95798-9002   Phone: (916) 322-4000 or (800) 952-5210
http://www.dca.ca.gov/bsis/bsispi.htm
Experience: Three years investigative work or equivalent. If a degree has been

earned, two years of experience is required. Must have attended a course dealing with power of arrest, caring and use of firearms, nightstick.

COLORADO—(NLR)—http://www.colorado.gov/
No longer requires a license.
Interested parties should contact their local police department.
Experience: None

CONNECTICUT—(SLR)—http://www.ct.gov/
Department of Public Safety, Division of State Police, Special License and Firearms Unit, State of Connecticut, 1111 Country Club Road, Middletown, CT 06450
Phone (860) 685-8160
http://www.state.ct.us/dps/SLFU/PrivateDetectivesHome.htm

DELAWARE—(SLR)—http://delaware.gov/
Delaware State Police, Detective Licensing, P.O. Box 430, Dover, DE 19903-0430
Phone: (302) 739-5900
http://www.state.de.us/dsp/sbi.htm#UCR
Experience: Five years as an investigator or as police officer with an organized police department in any state, county, municipality, or with any investigative agency in the USA.

DISTRICT OF COLUMBIA—(SLR)—http://www.state.dc.us/
District of Columbia, Security Officers Management Branch, Metro Police, Security Unit 2000, 14th St. NW, Washington, D.C. 20009
Phone: (202) 939-8722

FLORIDA—(SLR)—http://www.myflorida.com/
Division of Licensing, Bureau of License Issuance
P.O. Box 6687, Tallahassee, FL 32314-6687
Phone: (850) 488-5381
http://www.licgweb.doacs.state.fl.us/duties/issuance.html
Experience: Two years in performing the type of service permitted under the agency license for which applied. Class "C"—two years experience or training in one or a combination of more than one of the following: private investigative work or related fields, college course work, and seminars related to private investigation.

GEORGIA—(SLR)—http://www.georgia.gov/
Georgia Board of Private Detective and Security Agencies
166 Pryor Street, S.W., Atlanta, GA 30303-3465
Phone: (404) 656-2282   FAX: (404) 657-4220
http://www.sos.state.ga.us/plb/detective/

HAWAII—(SLR)— http://www.state.hi.us/
Hawaii State Government, Board of Private Detectives & Guards, DCCA, PVL, Licensing Branch, 1010 Richards Street, P.O. Box 541, Honolulu, HI 96801
Phone: (808) 587-3295 or (808) 586-2701/3000

http://www.state.hi.us/dcca/pvl/areas_private_detective.html
Experience: Four years employment with a private investigative firm, or employment as a police officer or as an investigator with a state or local agency.

IDAHO—(NLR)—http://www.accessidaho.org/index.html
State of Idaho, Office of Attorney General
7200 Barrister Drive, Boise, ID 83720-0010
Phone: (208) 334-2400   FAX: (208) 334-2530
Ada County requires licensing via Ada County Sheriff's Office
http://www.adasheriff.org/

ILLINOIS—(SLR)—http://www.illinois.gov/
Illinois Dept. of Professional Regulations
320 West Washington St., 3rd Floor, Springfield, IL 62786
Phone: (217) 782-8556 or (217) 785-0800
http://www.ildpr.com/WHO/dtct.asp
Experience: Minimum of three of last five years full-time for a licensed Private Investigative Agency or law-enforcement agency. If a degree is held, two of the last three years may be substituted.

INDIANA—(SLR)—http://www.state.in.us/
Indiana State Of, Professional Licensing Agency
Indiana Government Center South, 302 W. Washington Street, Room E034
Indianapolis, IN 46204-2700   Phone: (317) 232-2980   FAX: (317) 232-2312
http://www.in.gov/pla/bandc/detective/
Experience: Two years experience required in a related field.

IOWA—(SLR)—http://www.state.ia.us/
Administrative Services Division
Iowa Department of Public Safety, Wallace State Office Bldg., Des Moines, IA 50319
Phone: (515) 281-3211
http://www.state.ia.us/government/dps/iowacode/cd9780a.htm
Experience: No previous experience required.

KANSAS (SLR)—http://www.state.ks.us/
Kansas Bureau of Investigation
Office of the Attorney General, 1620 SW Tyler Street, Topeka, KS 66612
Phone: (785)-296-8200   FAX: (785) 296-0915
http://www.accesskansas.org/kbi/

KENTUCKY—(NLR)—http://www.kydirect.net/
Commonwealth of Kentucky, Justice Cabinet Office of the Secretary,
406 Wapping Street, Frankfort, KY 40601
Phone: (502) 564-4704
http://www.kpia.org/legislation.htm

LOUISANA—(SLR)—http://www.state.la.us/
Louisiana State Board of Private Investigator Examiners
2051 Silverside Drive, Suite 190, Baton Rouge, LA 70808

Phone: (225) 763-3556 or (800) 299-9696   FAX: (225) 763-3536
http://www.lsbpie.com/

MAINE—(SLR)—http://www.state.me.us/
Department of Public Safety,
Location: 397 Water Street, Gardiner, ME
Mail: 164 State House Station, Augusta, ME 04333-0164
Phone: (207) 624-8775
http://www.state.me.us/dps/lisc.htm or
http://janus.state.me.us/legis/statutes/32/title32ch89sec0.html

MARYLAND—(SLR)—http://www.state.md.us/
Correctional Services, Maryland State Police, PI Licensing Division, Jessup, MD
Phone: (410) 799-0191, ext. 331
http://www.inform.umd.edu/
Experience: Five years of related experience or three full years experience in an
investigative capacity or as a detective while serving as a police officer with an
organized police department.

MASSACHUSETTS—(SLR)—http://www.state.ma.us/
Massachusetts Department of State Police, Certification Unit
485 Maple Street, Danvers, MA 01923
Phone: (978) 538-6128   FAX: (978) 538-6021
http://www.state.ma.us/dps/ or http://www.lpdam.com/
Experience: Three years in a related field.

MICHIGAN—(SLR)—http://www.michigan.gov/
Department of Consumer & Industry Services
525 W. Ottawa, P.O. Box 30004, Lansing, MI 48909
Phone: (517) 241-5645 or (517) 373-1820   FAX: (517) 373-2129
http://www.michigan.gov/cis
Experience: Three years experience required.

MINNESOTA—(SLR)—http://www.state.mn.us/
Board of Private Detective and Protective Agent Services
445 Minnesota Street, St. Paul, MN 55101-5530
Phone: (651) 215-1753   Fax: (651) 296-7096
TTY Users: (651) 282-6555   e-mail: mn.pdb@state.mn.us
http://www.dps.state.mn.us/pdb/
Experience: Three year's experience in a related field.

MISSISSIPPI—(NLR)—http://www.state.ms.us/
None required

MISSOURI—(NLR)—http://www.state.mo.us/
P.O. Box 720, Jefferson City, MO 65102
Experience: None required on the state level
State law requires licensing in Kansas City and St Louis,
Joplin, St Joseph and Springfield.

MONTANA—(SLR)—http://www.state.mo.us/
Department of Public Safety
Private Detective & Protective Agent Services Board
444 Cedar Street, St. Paul, MN 55101   Phone: (612) 215-1753
http://www.discoveringmontana.com/css/default.asp
Experience: Three years related experience or degree in police administration.

NEBRASKA—(SLR)—http://www.state.ne.us/
Secretary of State, Suite 2300, State Capitol, Lincoln, NE 68509
Phone: (402) 471-2554   FAX: (402) 471-3237
http://www.nol.org/home/SOS/Privatedetectives/pd.htm
Experience: a minimum of 3000 hours of verifiable investigative experience.

NEVEDA—(SLR)—http://www.nv.gov/
Office of the Attorney General, Private Investigator's Licensing Board
100 N. Carson St. Carson City, NV 89701-4717   Phone: (775) 684-1147
http://ag.state.nv.us/Divisions/Fraudunits/Geninv/Pilb/pilb.htm
Experience: Repossession license: five years as repossession, or equivalent. Private patrolman: five years experience as private patrolman, or equivalent. Private investigator: five years experience, or the equivalent.

NEW HAMPSHIRE—(SLR)—http://www.state.nh.us/
Secretary - Permits and Licensing Unit
New Hampshire State Police, 10 Hazen Drive, Concord, NH 03305
Phone: (603) 271-3575   FAX: (603) 271-1153
Web Site: www.state.nh.us/nhsp/ or
http://www.nhes.state.nh.us/elmi/licertoccs/priva01.htm
Experience: Either an Associate of Science or Bachelor of Science in Criminal Justice and two years minimum employment as a licensed investigator; a minimum of four years as a full-time firefighter and certification by the International Association of Arson Investigators; a minimum of four years experience as a full-time law enforcement officer; or a minimum of four years employment as a full-time licensed private detective.

NEW JERSEY—(SLR)—http://www.state.nj.us/
State of New Jersey, Department of Law and Public Safety
New Jersey State Police, Box 7068, West Trenton, NJ 08625
Phone: (609) 882-2000
http://www.state.nj.us/lps/njsp/ or http://www.njsp.org/feedback.html
Experience: At least five years experience as investigator or police officer with organized police department, or with an investigative agency of the United States, or state, county, or municipality.

NEW MEXICO—(SLR)—http://www.state.nm.us/
Private Investigator and Polygraph Board
2055 Pacheco Street, Suite 400, P.O. Box 25101, Santa Fe, NM 87504-5101
Phone: (505)476-7080   FAX: (505) 476-7095
http://www.rld.state.nm.us/b&c/pipolygraph/index.htm

Experience: Private patrol: two years Private investigator: three years of last five involved in investigative work.

NEW YORK—(SLR)—http://www.state.ny.us/
New York State Department of State, Division of Licensing Services
84 Holland Avenue, Albany, NY 12208-3490
Phone: (518) 474-4429   FAX: (518) 473-6648
http://www.dos.state.ny.us/lcns/licensing.html
Experience: Three years for PI license; two years for watch/guard.

NORTH CAROLINA—(SLR)—http://www.state.nc.us/
Private Protective Services Of North Carolina
Post Office Box 29500, 3320 Old Garner Rd, Raleigh, NC 27626-0500
Phone: (919) 875-3611   FAX: (919) 875-3609
http://www.jus.state.nc.us/pps/
Experience: For investigator's license: three years of investigative experience in the last five years, or at least two years experience within the last five years in an investigative capacity as a member of any federal or state, or county law enforcement agency, or sheriff's department.

NORTH DAKOTA—(SLR)—http://www.state.nd.us/
North Dakota Private Investigative & Security Board
P.O. Box 7026, Bismarck, ND 58505   Phone: (701) 222-3063
Experience: No rules and regulations govern related work experience for private investigator applicants.

OHIO—(SLR)—http://www.com.state.oh.us/
The Ohio Department of Commerce
Division of Real Estate and Professional Licensing
77 South High Street, 20th Floor, Columbus, OH 43215-6133
Phone: (614) 466-4100 or (614) 466-4130
Email: REPLD@com.state.oh.us
http://www.com.state.oh.us/ODOC/real/pisgmain.htm
Experience: Three years in a related field with a detective agency, law-enforcement agency, etc.

OKLAHOMA—(SLR)—http://www.state.ok.us/
Council on Law Enforcement, Education & Training
Private Security Division, P. O. Box 11476 Cimarron Station
Oklahoma City, OK 73136-0476
http://www.cleet.state.ok.us/Private_Security.htm
Experience: No specific experience requirements. Applicant's experience as a private detective with an agency or related field will be considered.

OREGON—(SLR)—http://www.oregon.gov/
Department of State Police, Oregon Board of Investigators
445 State Office Bldg., 800 NE Oregon Street #33, Portland, OR 97232
Phone: (503) 731-4359   FAX: (503) 731-4366
http://landru.leg.state.or.us/ors/703.html

Experience: Must have at least 1,500 hours of experience in investigatory work or have completed a related course of study approved by the board.

PENNSYLVANIA—(BLR)—http://www.state.pa.us/
Pennsylvania Association of Licensed Investigators
P.O. Box 60036, Harrisburg, PA 17106-0036
Phone: (717) 576-2253   FAX: (717) 233-5340
http://www.pali.org/
Experience: In sum, you must have experience as a law enforcement officer, or demonstrate proficiency and experience in topics defined under this Act.

PUERTO RICA—(SLR)—http://www.state.pr.us/
State Dept. & Police Dept., GPO Box 70166, San Juan, PR 00936
Phone: (787) 793-1234
http://www.estado.gobierno.pr/

RHODE ISLAND—(NLR)—http://www.state.ri.us/
State of Rhode Island, Providence Plantations
345 Harris Ave., Providence, RI 29221
Phone: (402) 277-2000
http://ww2 rilin.state.ri.us/generallaws/title5/5%2D5/s00003.htm
Experience: Not required

SOUTH CAROLINA—(SLR)—http://www.state.sc.us/
Law Enforcement Division, Broad River Rd, Box 21398, Columbia, SC 29221
Phone: (803) 737-9000
http://www.lpitr.state.us/bil95-96/507.htm
Experience: Minimum two years as a licensed detective agency, or two years of experience as a supervisor or administrator in industrial security of with a licensed private security agency, or two years with the FBI or a police department.

SOUTH DAKOTA—(NLR)—http://www.state.sd.us/
No P.I. license, but business license through Department of Revenue required.
http://www.state.sd.us/state/executive/attorney/attorney.html

TENNESSEE—(SLR)—http://www.state.tn.us/
Department of Commerce & Insurance
Private Protective Services Division, 500 James Robertson Parkway,
Nashville, TN 37243-1158
Phone: (615) 741-6382
http://www.state.tn.us/commerce/sec-indust/ PI&Poly/pi.htm
Experience: None required

TEXAS—(SLR)—http://www.state.tx.us/
Texas Commission of Private Security
4616 Howard Lane, Suite 140, Austin, TX 78728
Phone: (512) 238-5858   FAX: (512) 238-5853
http://www.tcps.state.tx.us/pi Page.htm
Experience: Three years of related experience. Manager must have two years of

supervisory experience.

UTAH—(SLR)—http://www.state.ut.us/
Utah Department of Public Safety
Division of Criminal Investigations & Technical Services
Bureau of Criminal Identification, 4501 South 2700 West, Salt Lake City, UT 84119
Phone (801) 965-4461/4445/4485
Mail: Box 148280, Salt Lake City, UT 84114-8280
http://www.bci.utah.gov/BailPI/PIHome.html
VERMONT—(SLR)—http://www.vermont.gov/
Board of Private Investigative
Armed Security Services, Office of Professional Regulation
109 State St., Montpelier, VT 05609-1101
Phone: (802) 828-2837
http://www.vtprofessionals.org/opr1/investigators/
Experience: Two years of related experience.

VIRGINIA—(SLR)—http://www.vipnet.org/comsportal/
Department of Criminal Justice Services
805 East Broad Street, 10th Floor, Richmond, VA 23219
Phone (804) 786-4000
http://www.infor.dcjs.state.va.us/ps/directory/businessSearch.cfm
Experience: Must have been employed in investigative or supervisory capacity in private security services business for three years.

WASHINGTON—(SLR)—http://access.wa.gov/
Department of Licensing, Master License Service
P.O. Box 9034, Olympia, WA 98507-9034
Phone: (360) 664-6611   FAX: (360) 570-7888
E-mail: Security@dol.wa.gov
http://www.dol.wa.gov/ppu/pifront.htm

WEST VIRGINIA—(SLR)—http://www.state.wv.us/
West Virginia Secretary of State, Licensing Division
The State Capitol—Private Investigator Licensing
Charleston, WV 25301
http://www.wvsos.com/licensing/piguard/main.htm
Experience: Three years private detective, investigator or member of a US government investigative service, a sheriff or member of a city or state police department or at least one year of training in investigative work at an accredited state college or university. Credit also given for Bachelors and Masters Degrees, extension and correspondence institutions or at least one year of supervised training in investigative industry with a licensed private detective agency.

WISCONSIN—(SLR)—http://www.wisconsin.gov/state/home/
State of Wisconsin, Dept of Regulation & Licensing
Wisconsin Accounting Examining Board
1400 East Washington Avenue, P. O. Box 8935, Madison, WI 53708-8935

Email: web@drl.state.wi.us
Phone: (608) 266-5511   FAX: (608) 267-0644
http://www.drl.state.wi.us/Regulation/applicant_information/dod124.html

WYOMING—(NLR)—http://www.state.wy.us/
Secretary of State, Joseph B. Meyer State Capitol Building
Cheyenne, WY 82002
Phone: (307) 777-7378   FAX: (307) 777-6217
http://soswy.state.wy.us/ or http://attorneygeneral.state.wy.us/dci/text_pifaq.html
Experience: No, but some municipalities may regulate private investigators and security alarm companies via city ordinance. You should check with the municipalities where you will conduct business.

ABOUT THE AUTHOR

William F. Mitchell, Jr., accomplished author and private investigator, was featured on NBC *Today Show* with Matt Lauer in a segment entitled "Unfaithfully Yours", CBS *The Early Show* in the segment entitled "Dating Again," Warner Brothers pilot of "The Larry Elder Show" and numerous talk radio shows across the country. He contributed to the segment "Why Men Cheat" on the "Dr. Phil Show." His quotes were featured in *Chicago Tribune* and *Esquire Magazine*.

Time Magazine heralded Mr. Mitchell's bold efforts in cracking the FBI's first major computer crime in 1978. Mitchell was the initial investigator in this landmark case. At Former FBI Agents' Conventions, ex-FBI Director William Webster boasted of this major accomplishment on numerous occasions. Mr. Mitchell proudly follows in the footsteps of his father, William F. Mitchell, Sr., a former FBI Agent serving under the genius of J. Edgar Hoover, Former Director of the FBI.

Mr. Mitchell embarked on a private investigative career now spanning three decades. Faced with an array of challenging assignments his adventures included complex civil and criminal cases. His extraordinary vocation included the apprehension of organized crime figures, reuniting lost family members, tracking down heirs to amazing fortunes, contributing to the triumphant apprehension of a parental fugitive named on the FBI's Most Wanted Parental Abduction List, recovering thousands of dollars in stolen property, risky undercover assignments and innumerable hours of surveillance. While facing dangerous situations Mr. Mitchell attributes his longevity to "quick thinking."

His career includes security manager positions for such Fortune 500 companies as GE and RCA protecting our "nation's secrets." He directed the second largest uniformed security guard operation in the nation.

Since 1987 Mr. Mitchell has been licensed in the state of New York. He has also practiced in Maryland, New Jersey, Pennsylvania, Washington, D.C. and Virginia. He has handled cases for clients from around the world.

In every case he strives to uncover truth, counsels clients and helps bring closure to those in the midst of an adulterous crisis. His investigative work and courtroom testimonies have led to countless favorable legal decisions and out-of-court settlements.

Mr. Mitchell's Bachelor's Degree in Psychology was awarded by Mt. St. Mary's College. In 1985 he achieved the prestigious Facility Security Officer Certification from the Department of Defense, as well as numerous certifications in security education. Adding to his skills and talents Mitchell earned certification as a P.S.E. (Psychological Stress Evaluator—voice stress device) examiner in lie detection through Dektor Counterintelligence of Springfield, Virginia in 1978. He was an original member of the now defunct ISSA (International Society of Stress Analysts).

Mr. Mitchell holds memberships with ALDONYS (Associated Licensed Detectives of New York State, Inc.), ION (Investigators online Network), and NAIS (National Association of Investigative Specialists). He is currently working on several new books stemming from past case assignments and associations with government agencies.

Mitchell earned the rank of Eagle Scout in Boy Scouts of America at age 14, and he continues to hold dear those values and skills learned in his youth. He resides in upstate New York with his lovely wife and four wonderful children. Since the release of his latest book, *If You Only Knew*, Mr. Mitchell has been referred to as "the Dr. Phil of private detectives."